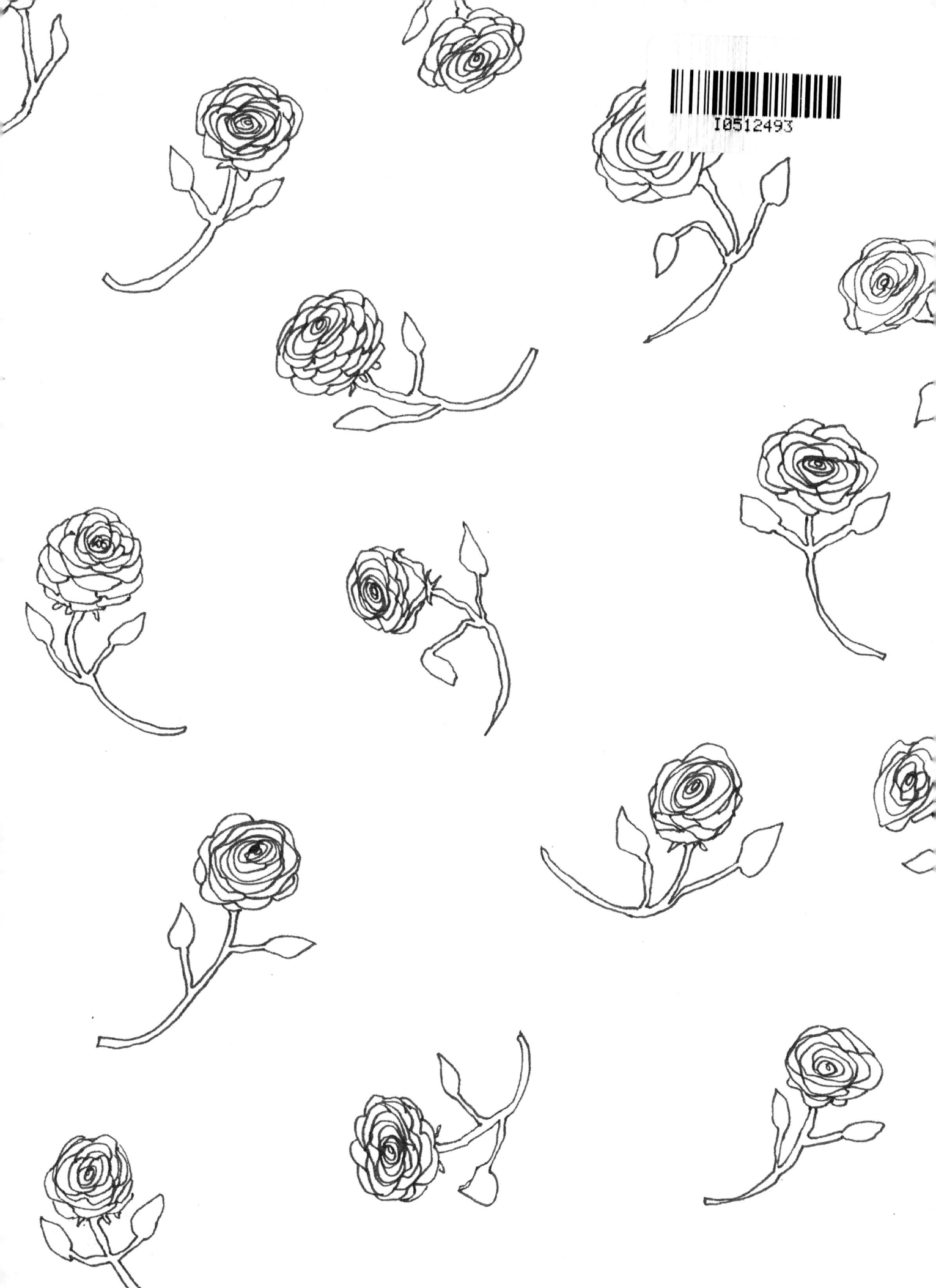

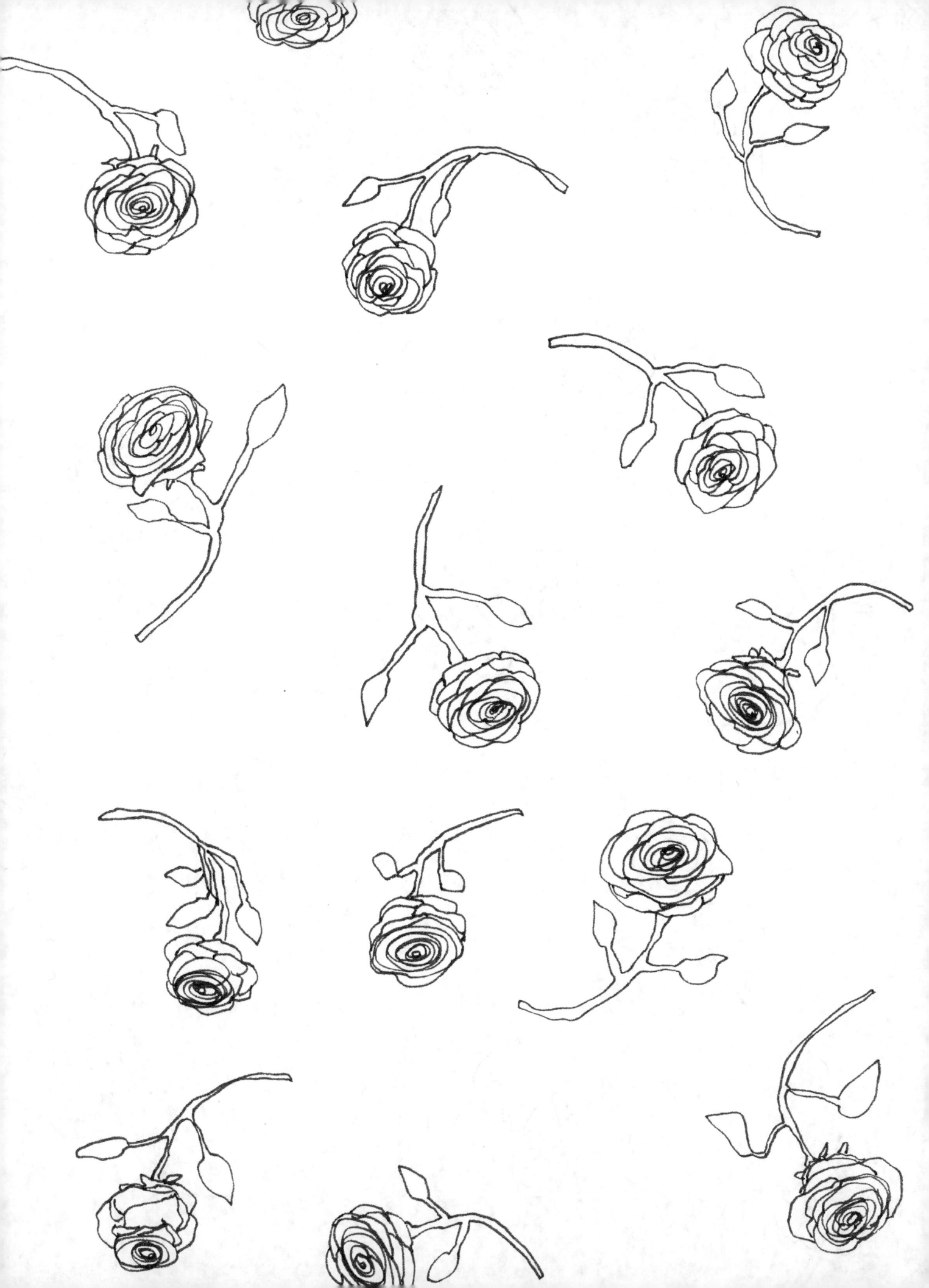

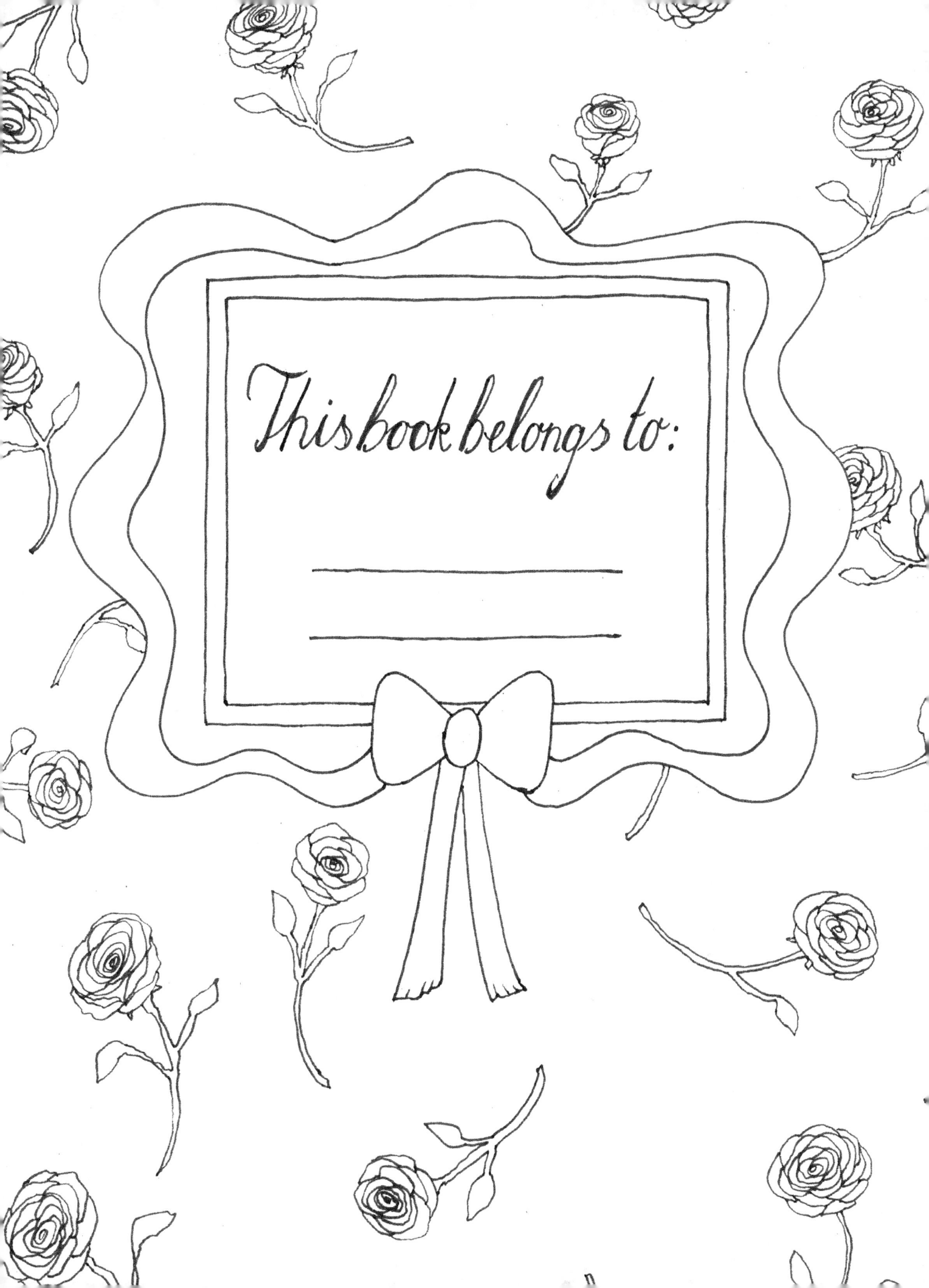

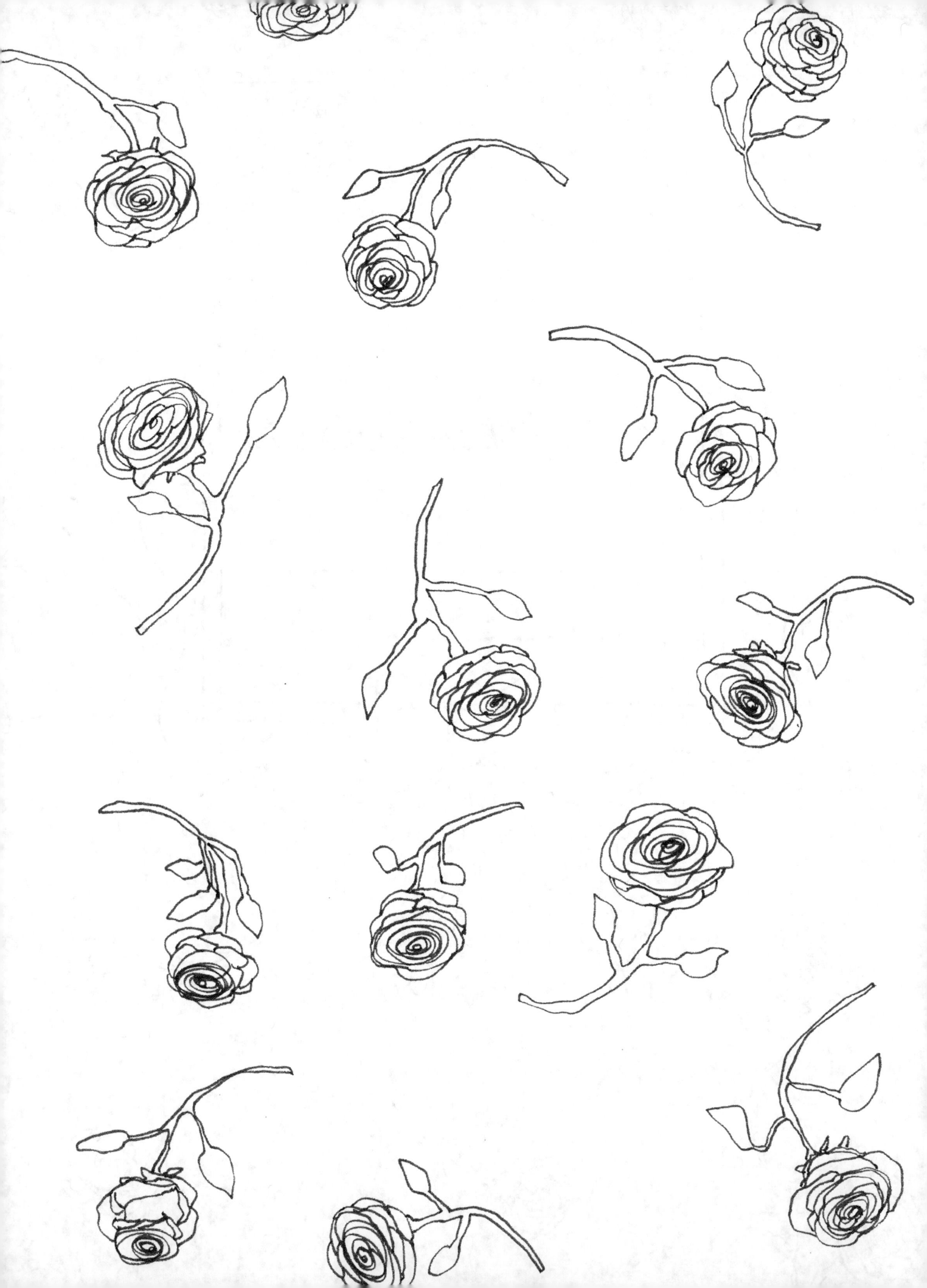

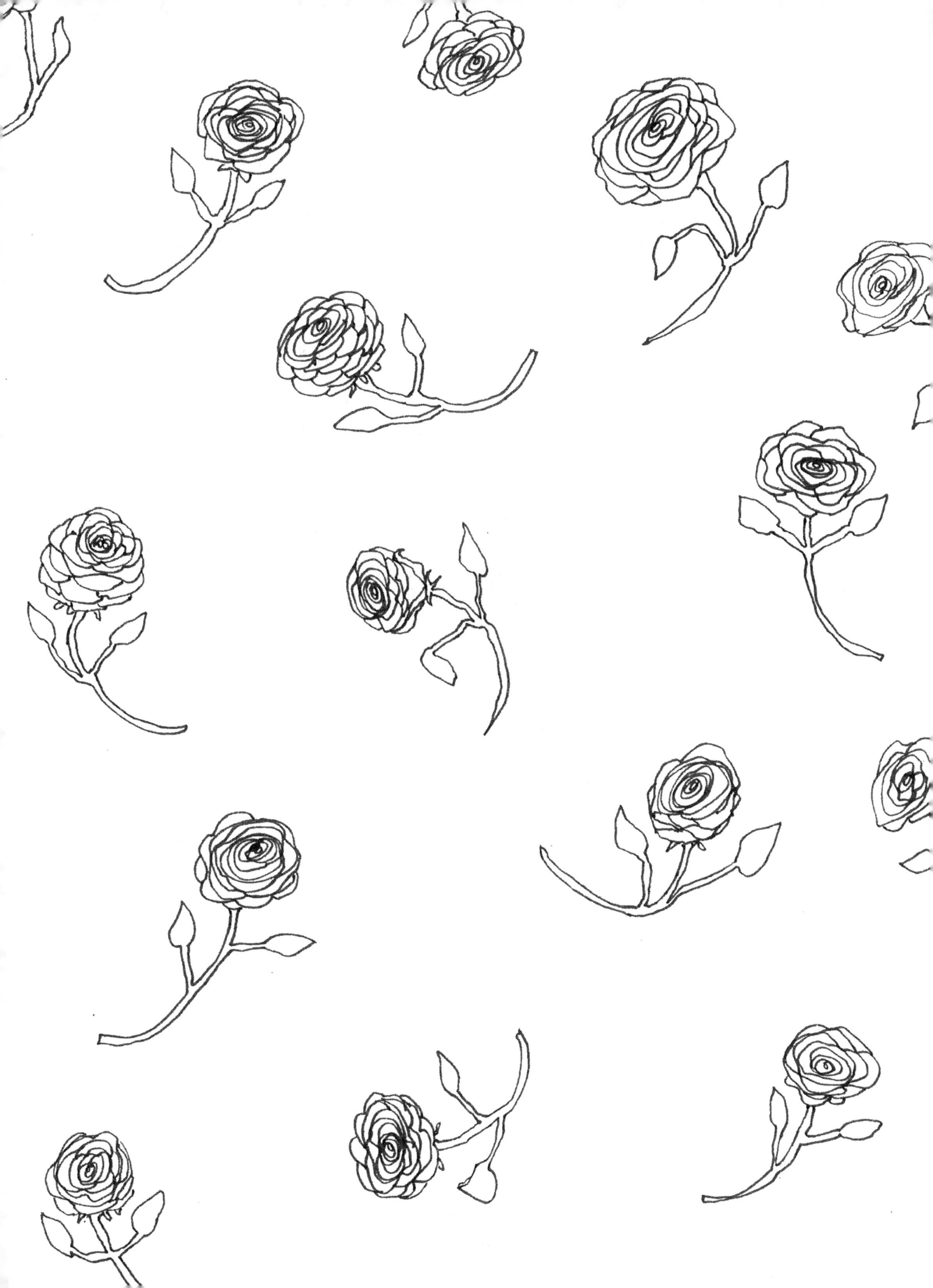

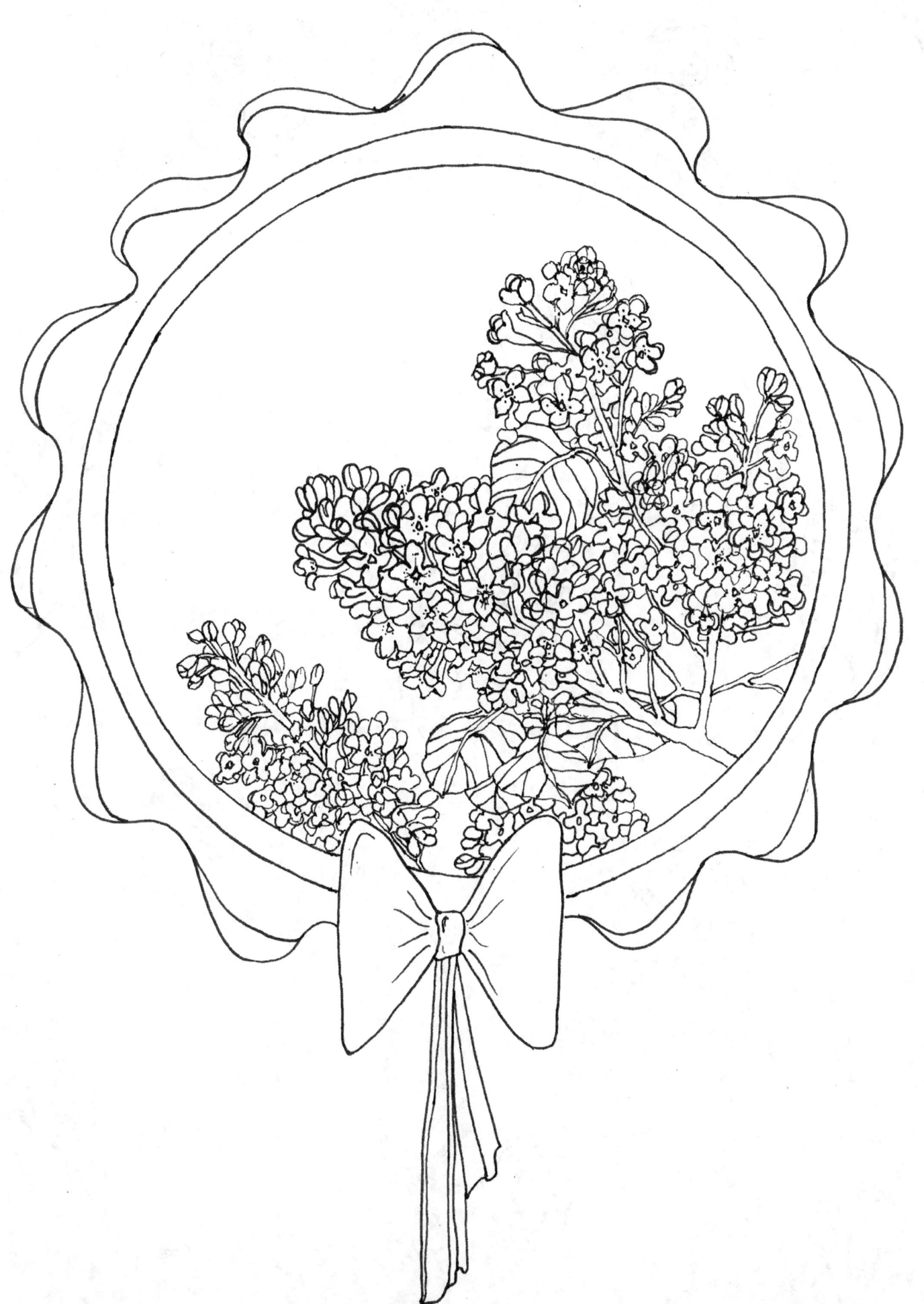

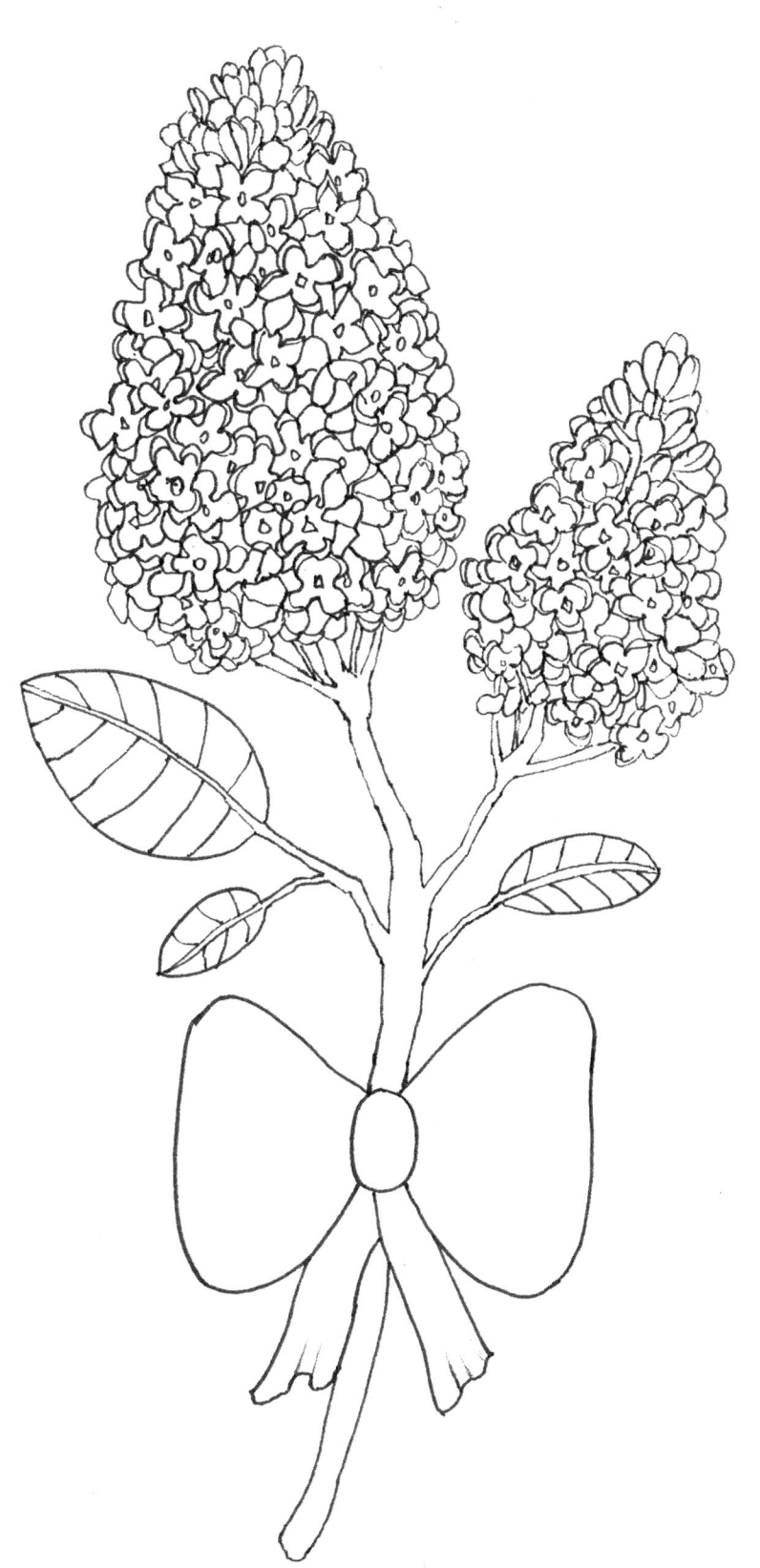

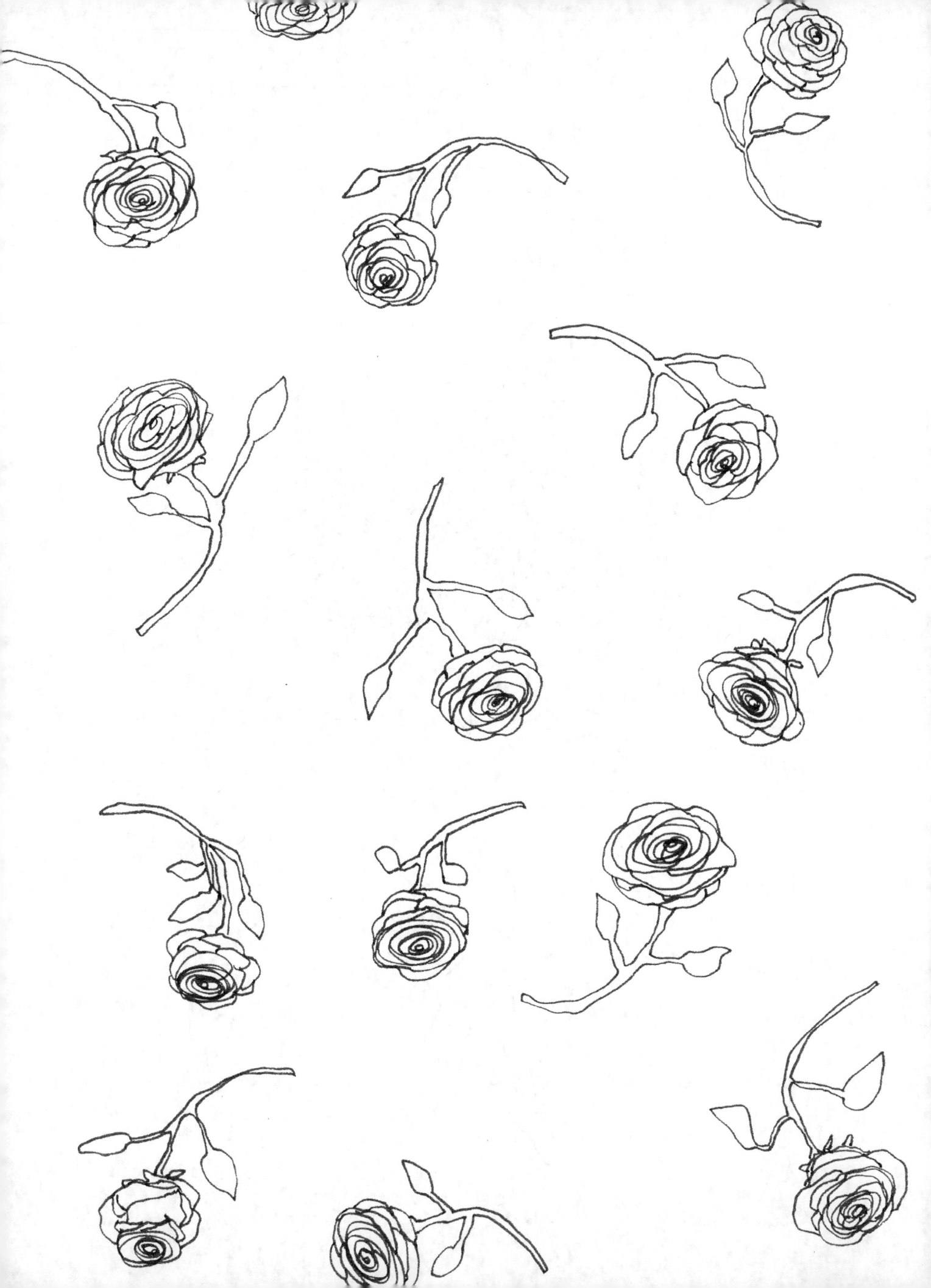

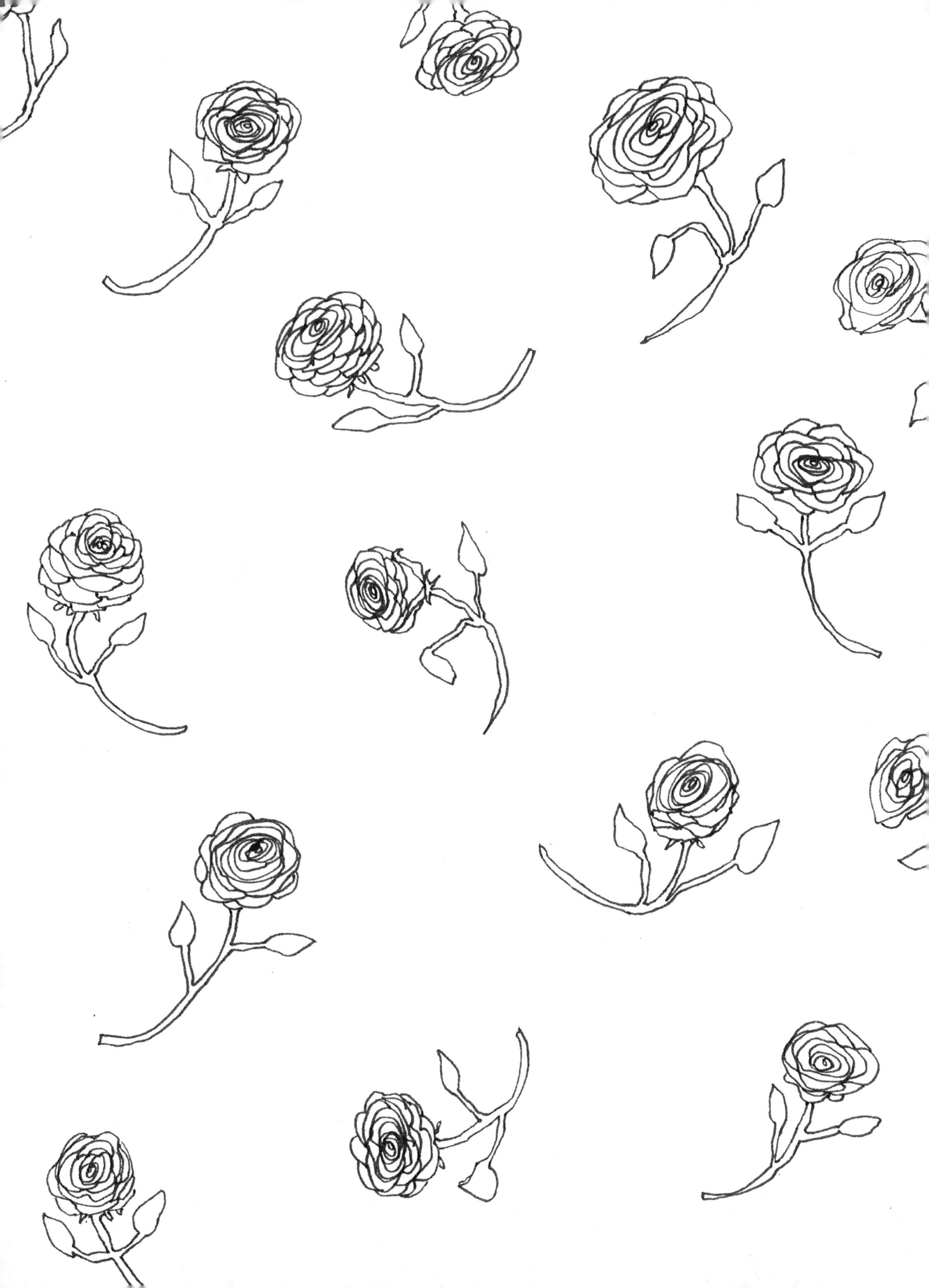

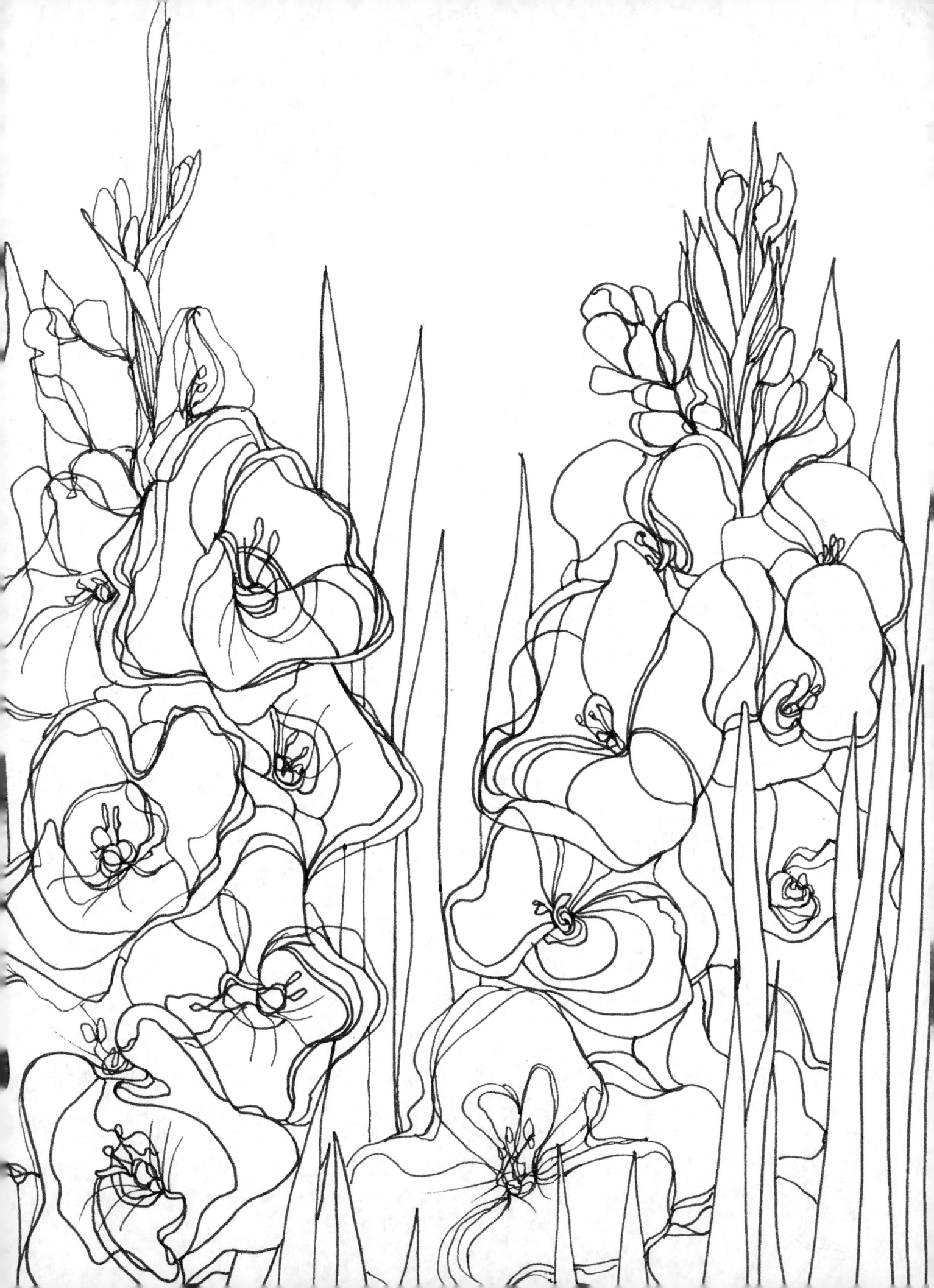

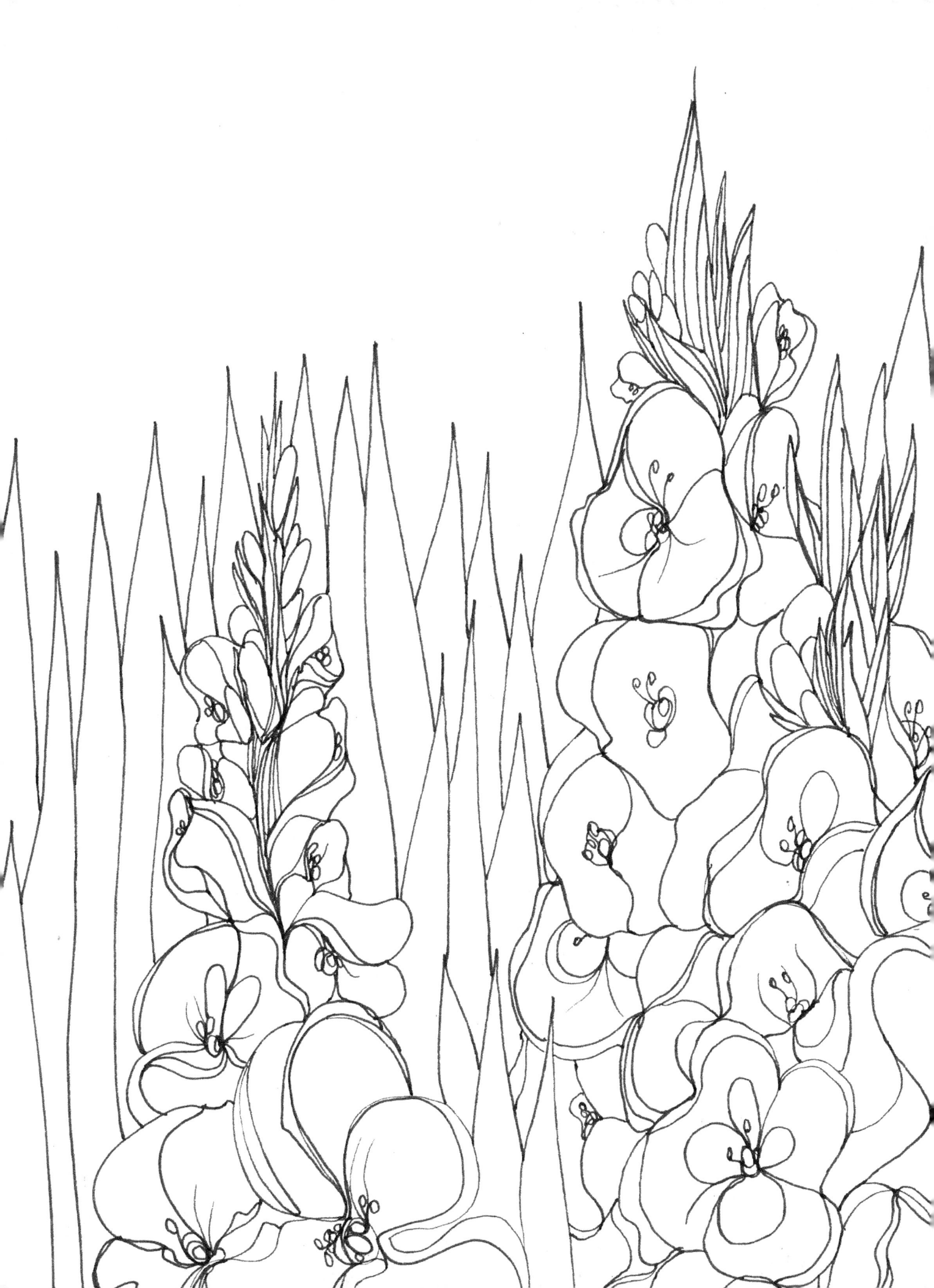

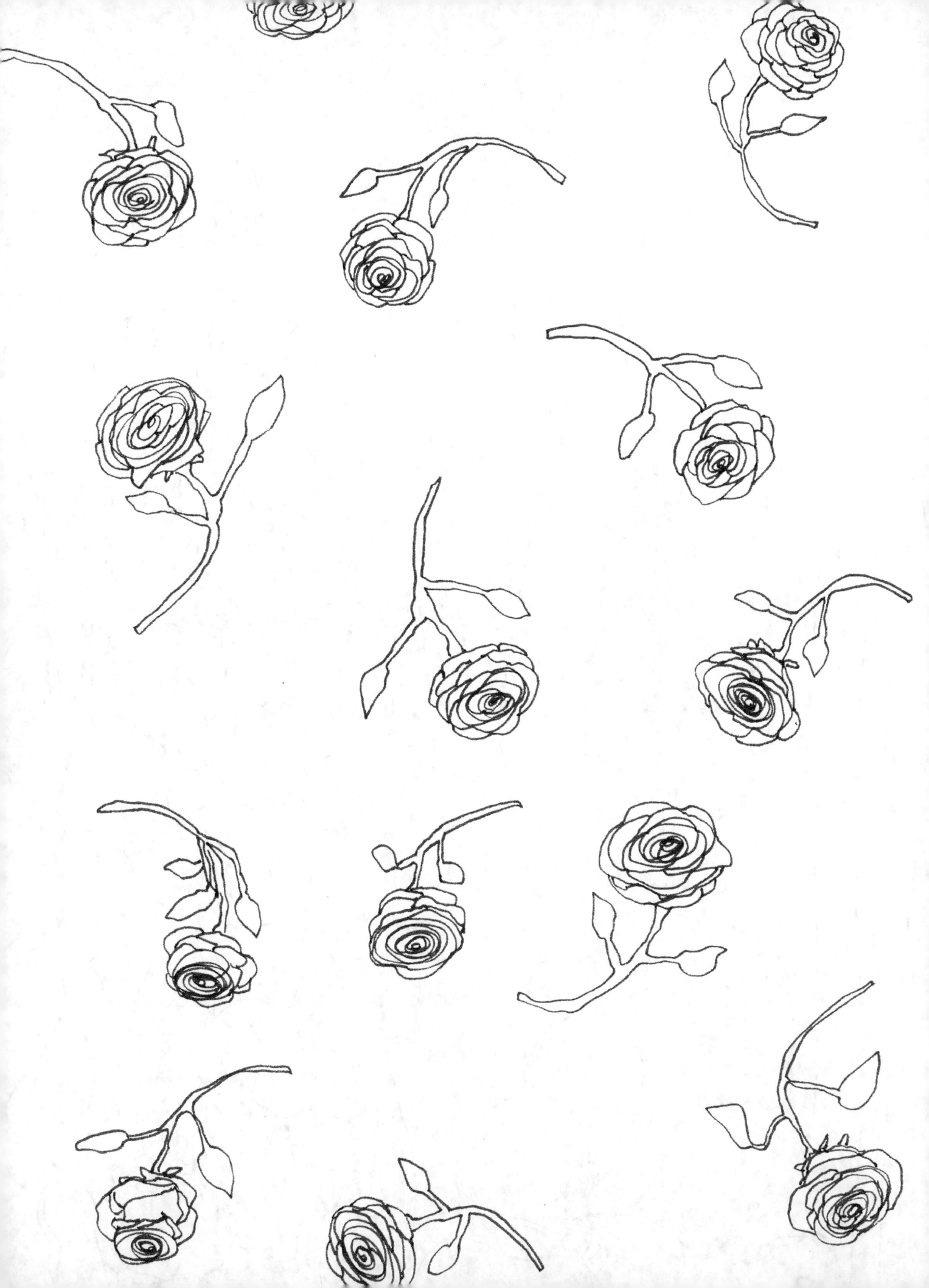

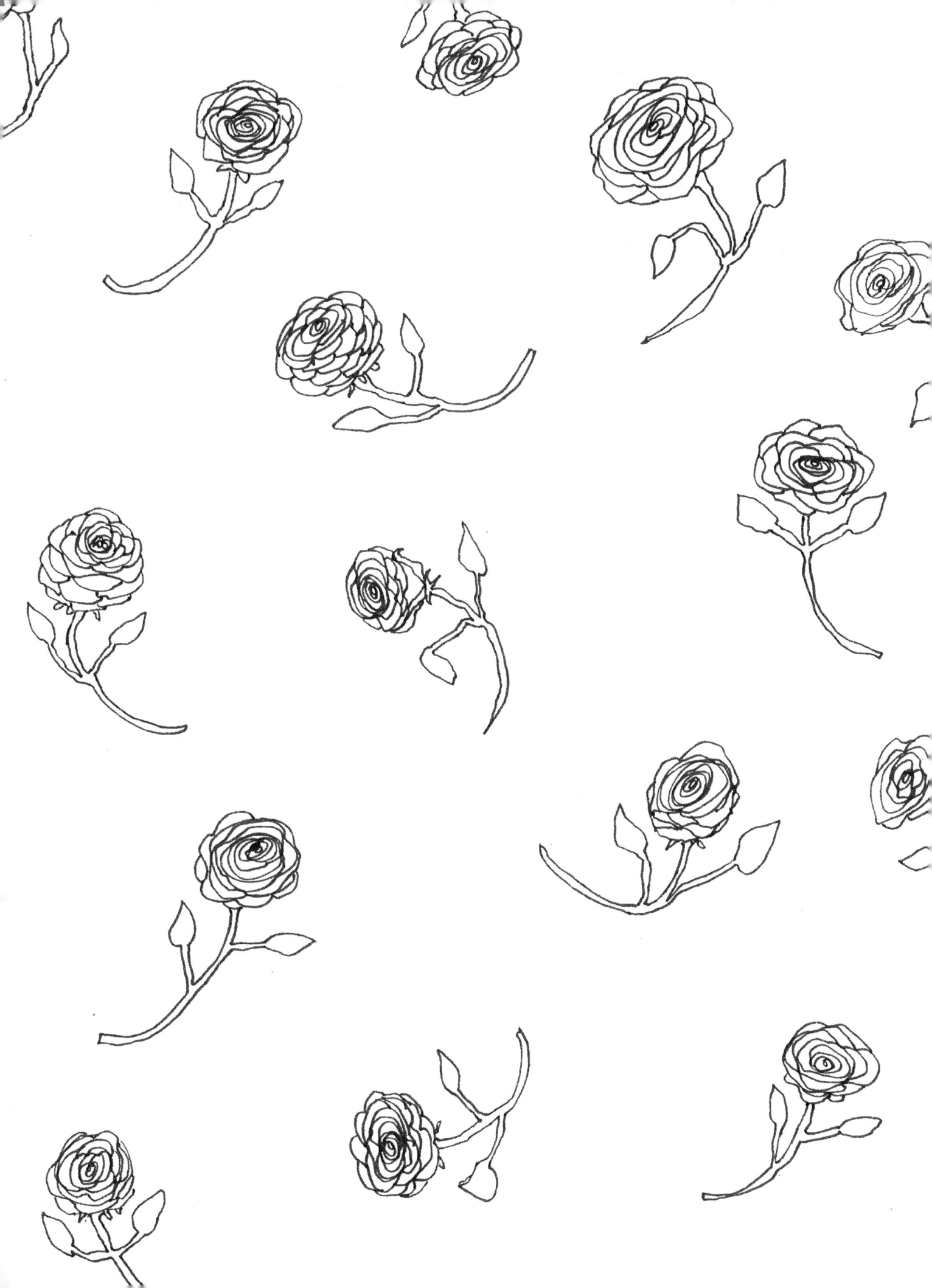

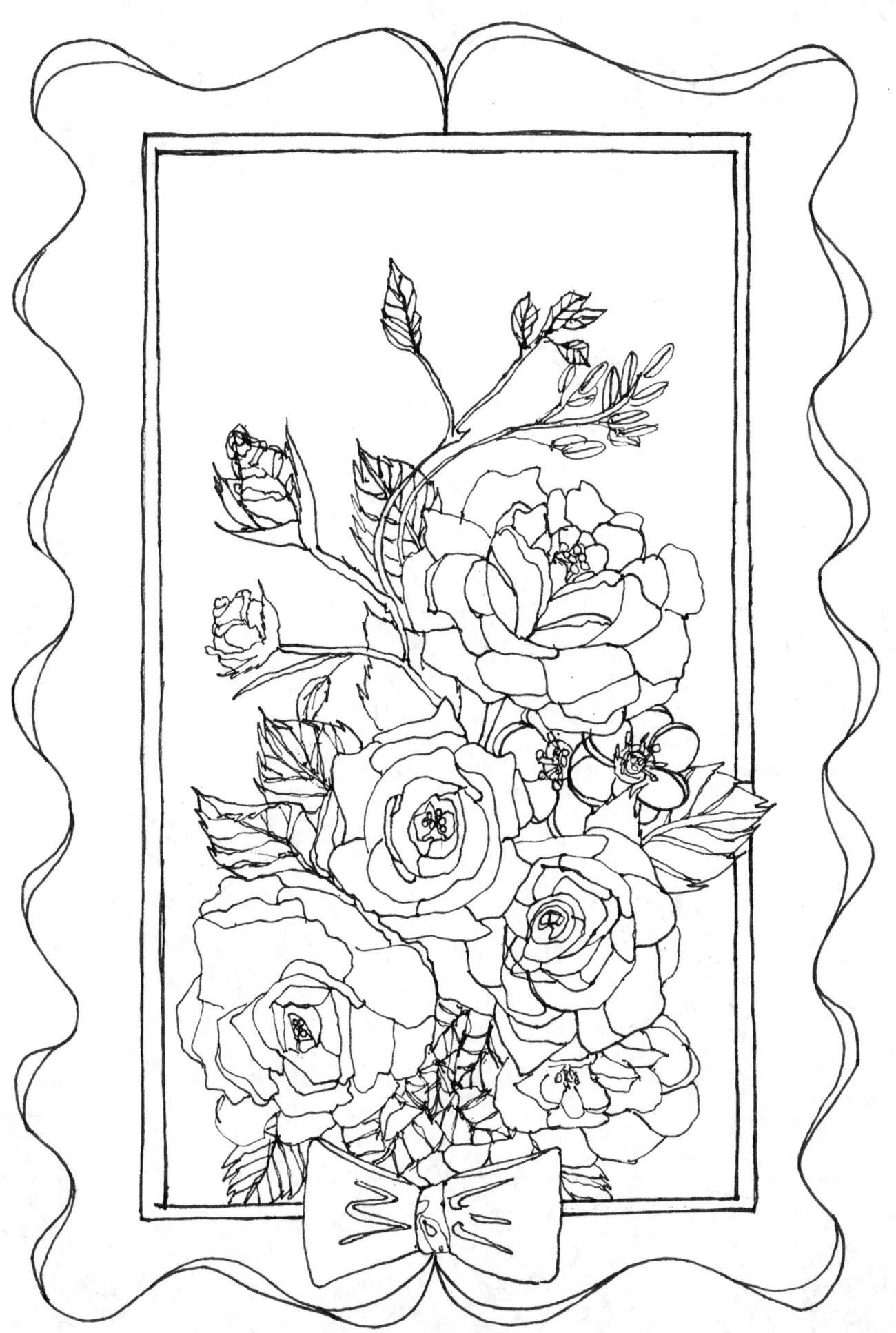

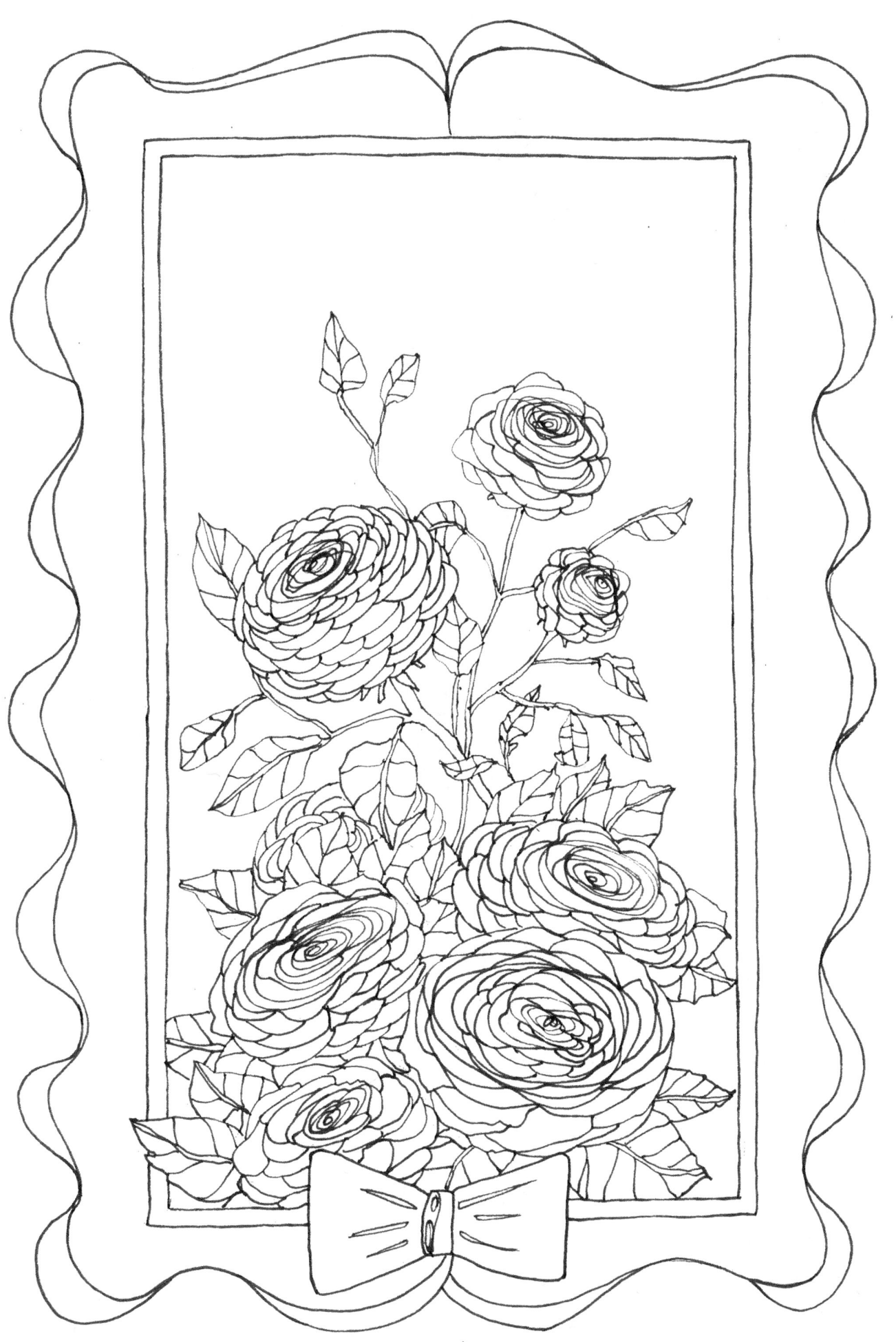

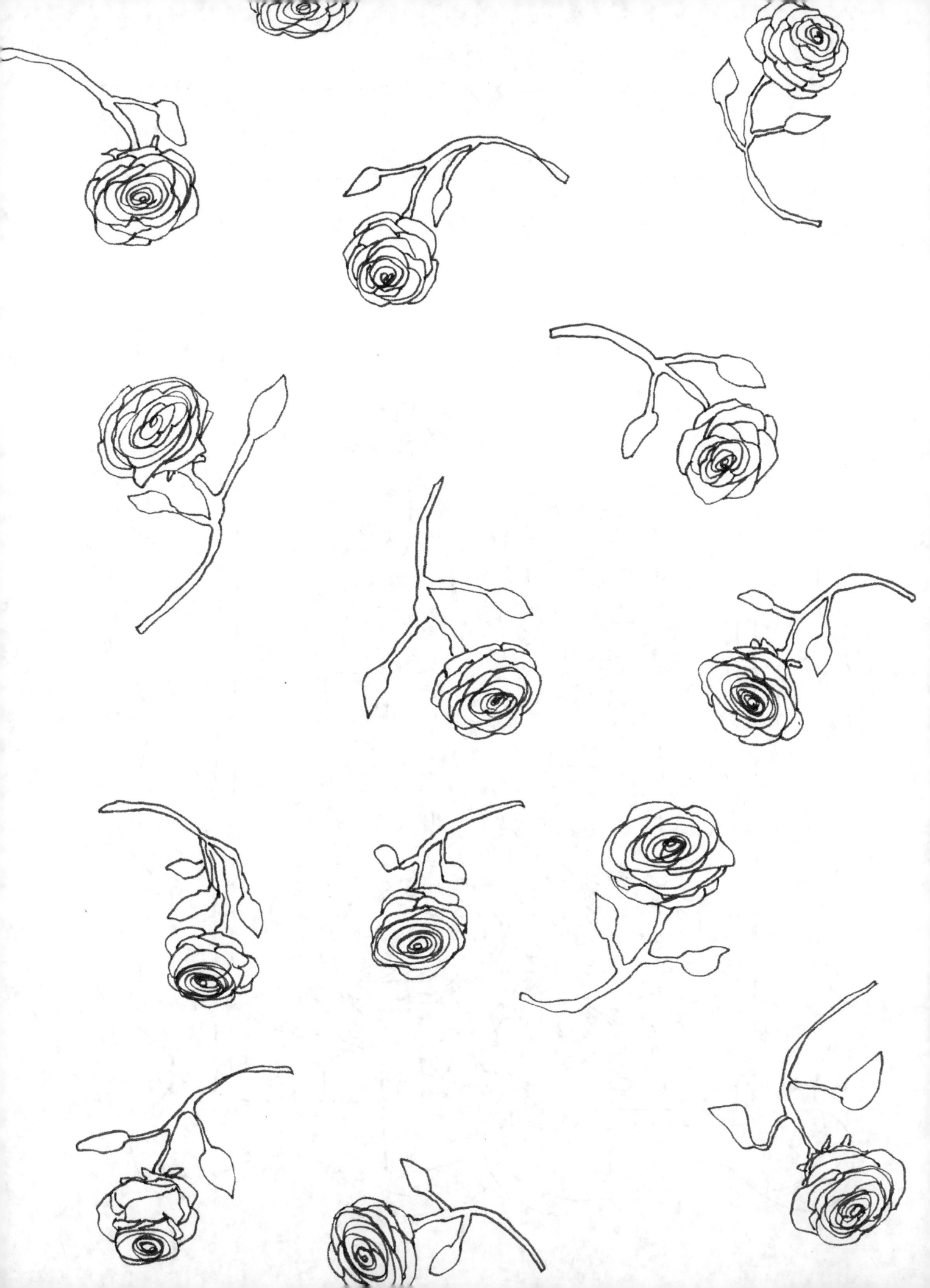

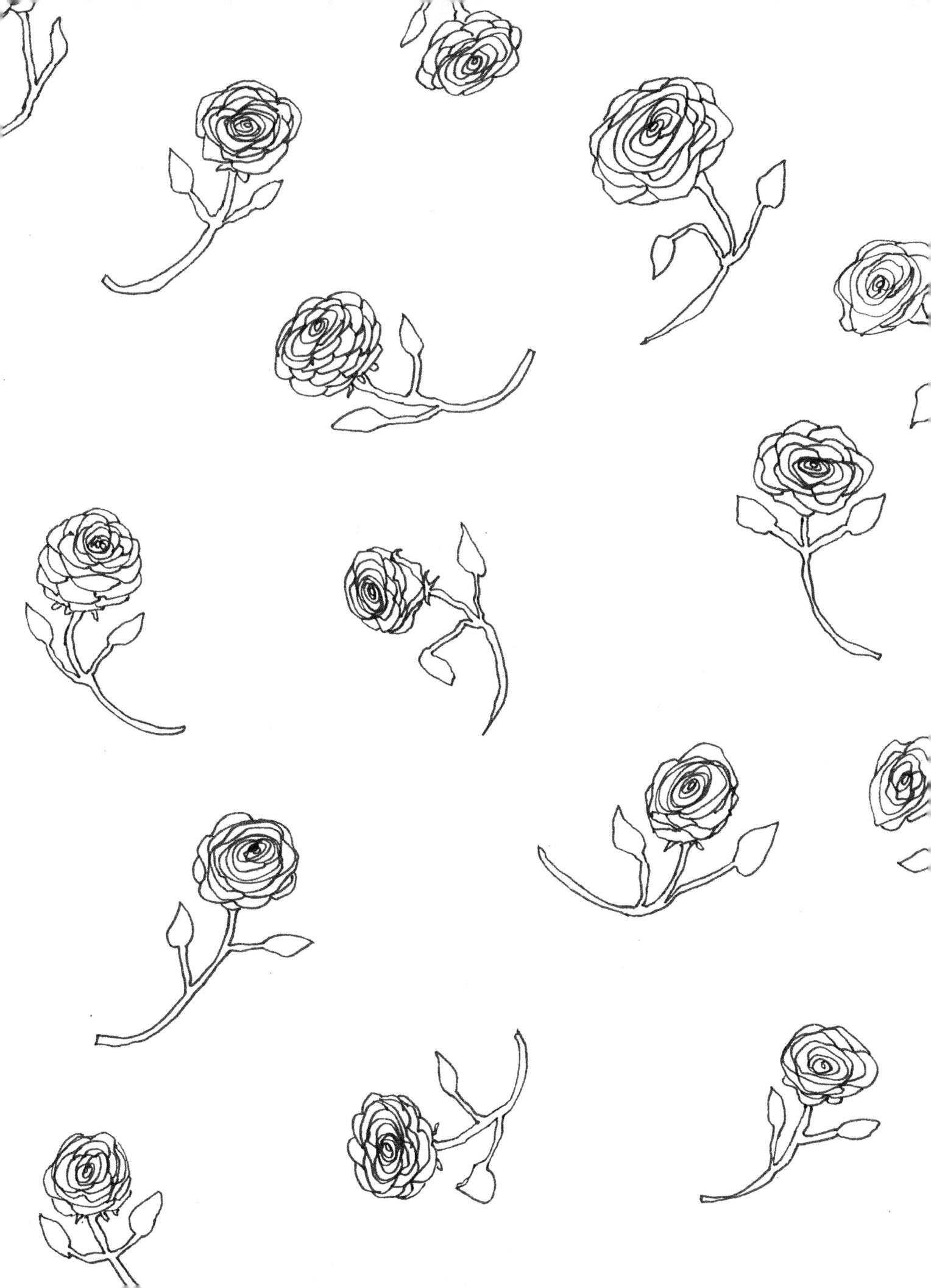

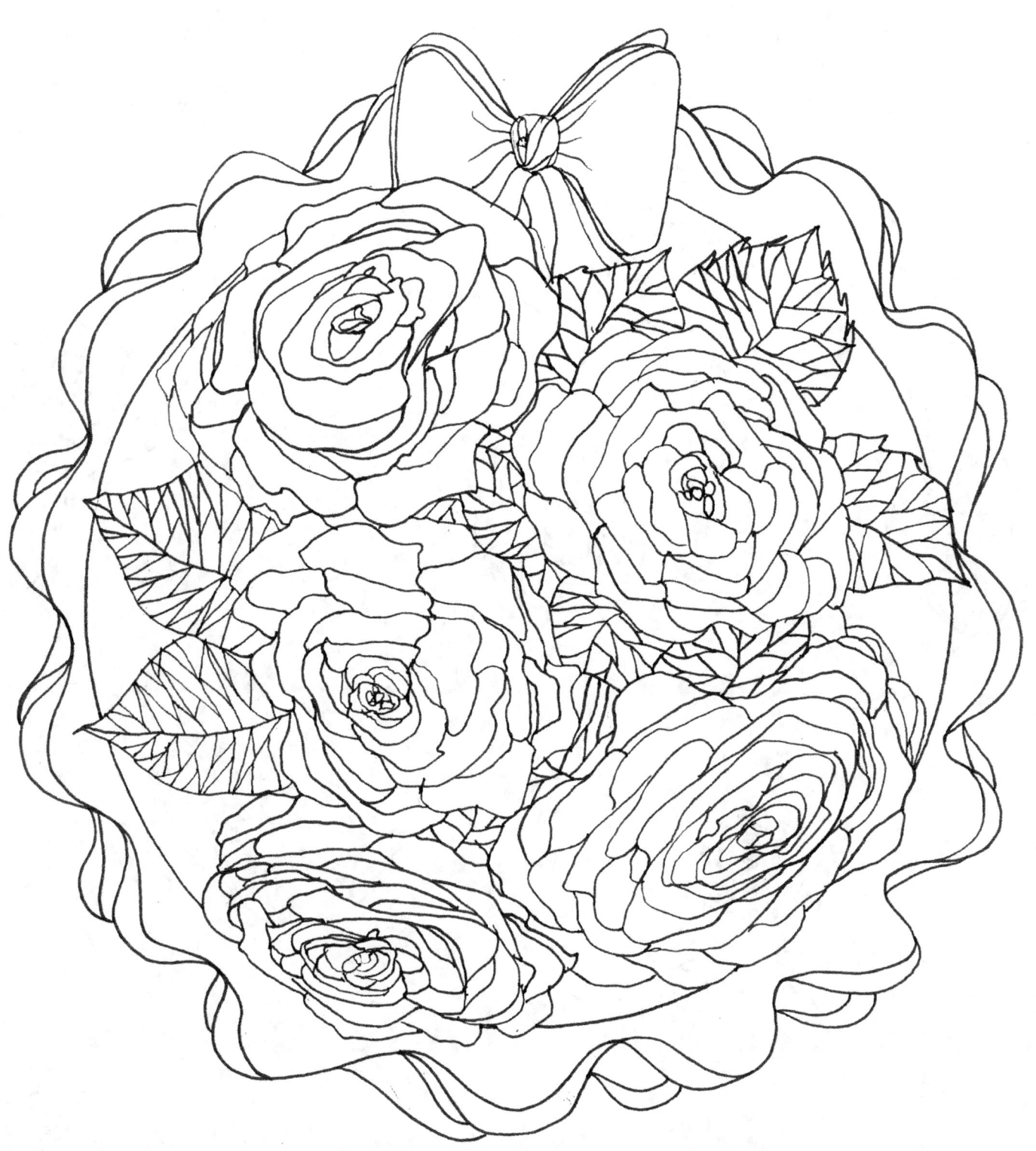

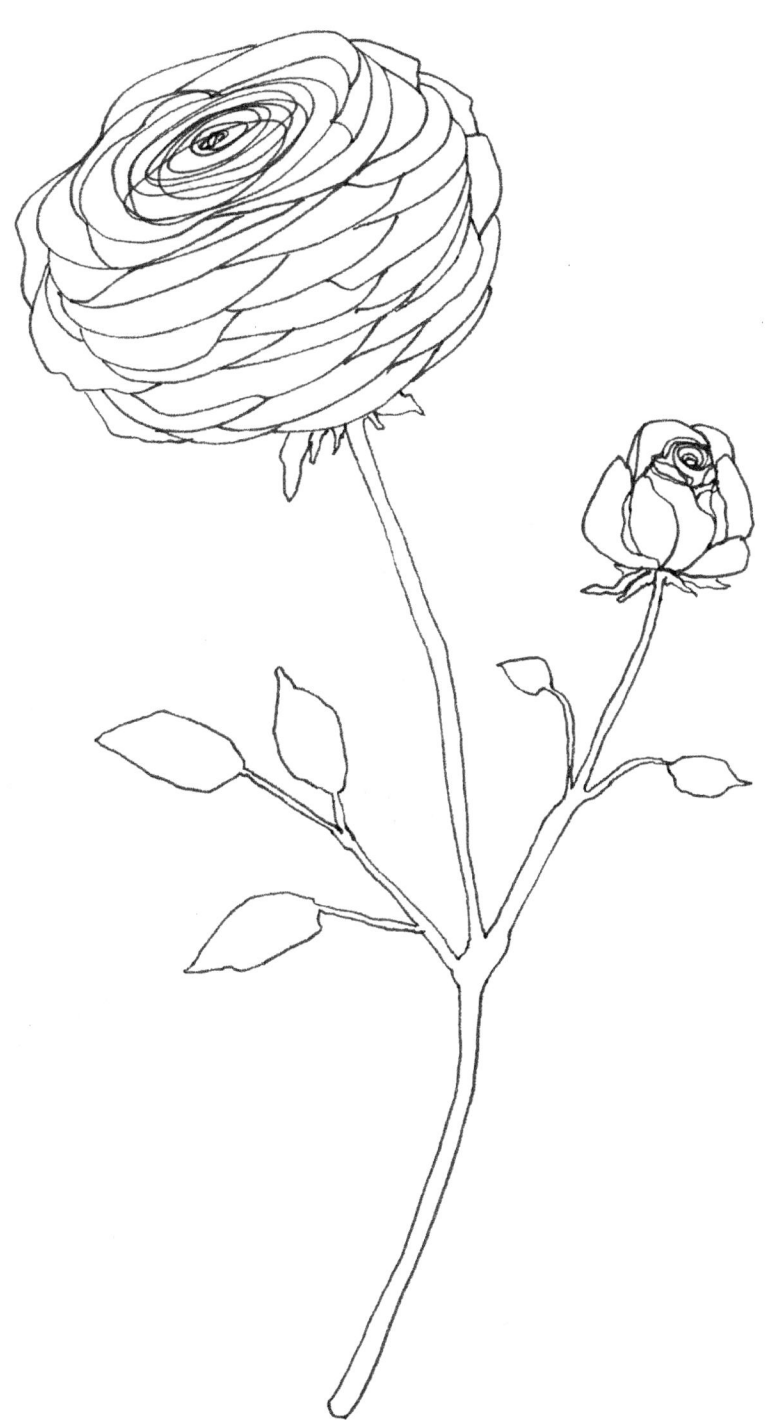

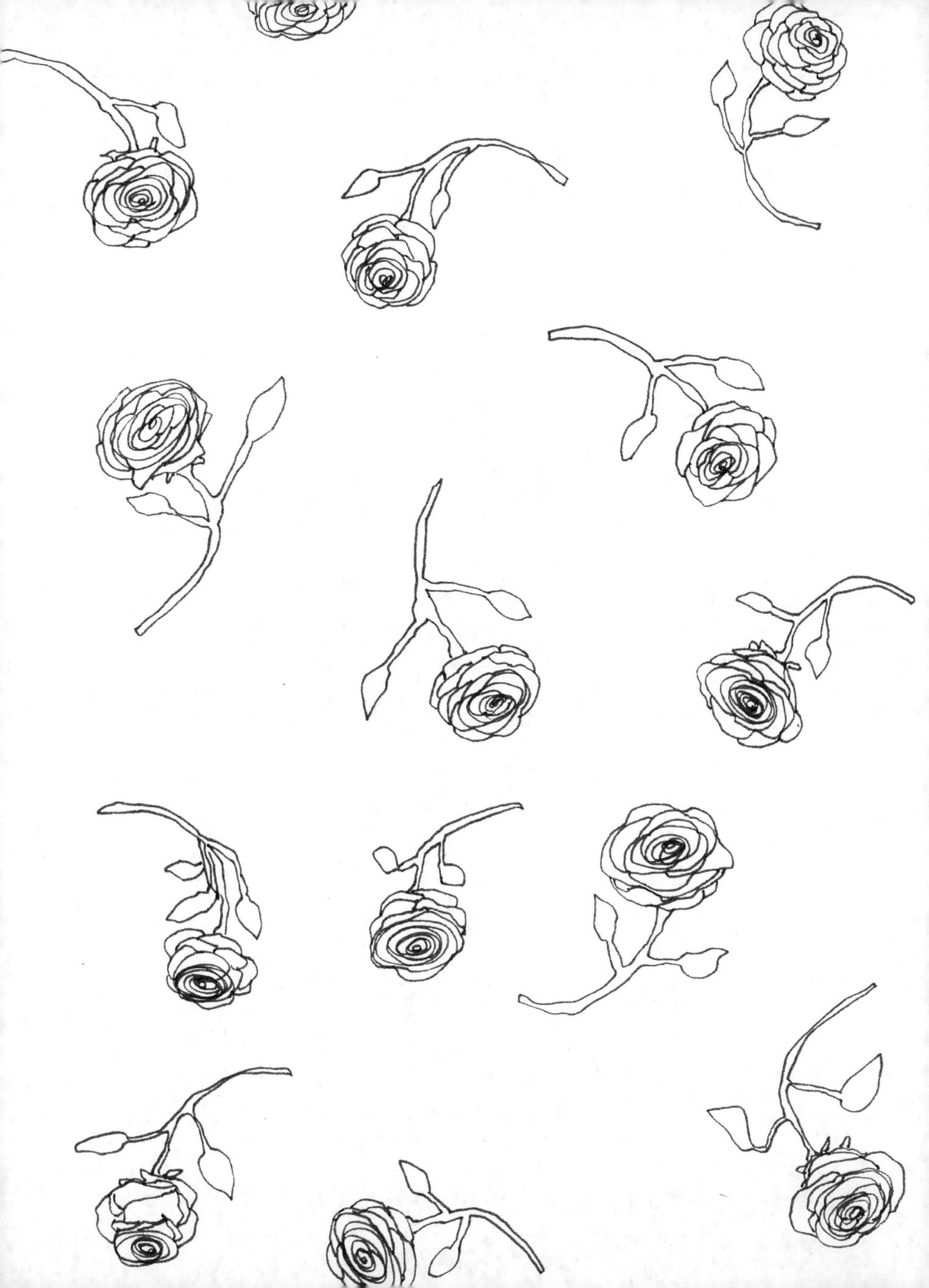

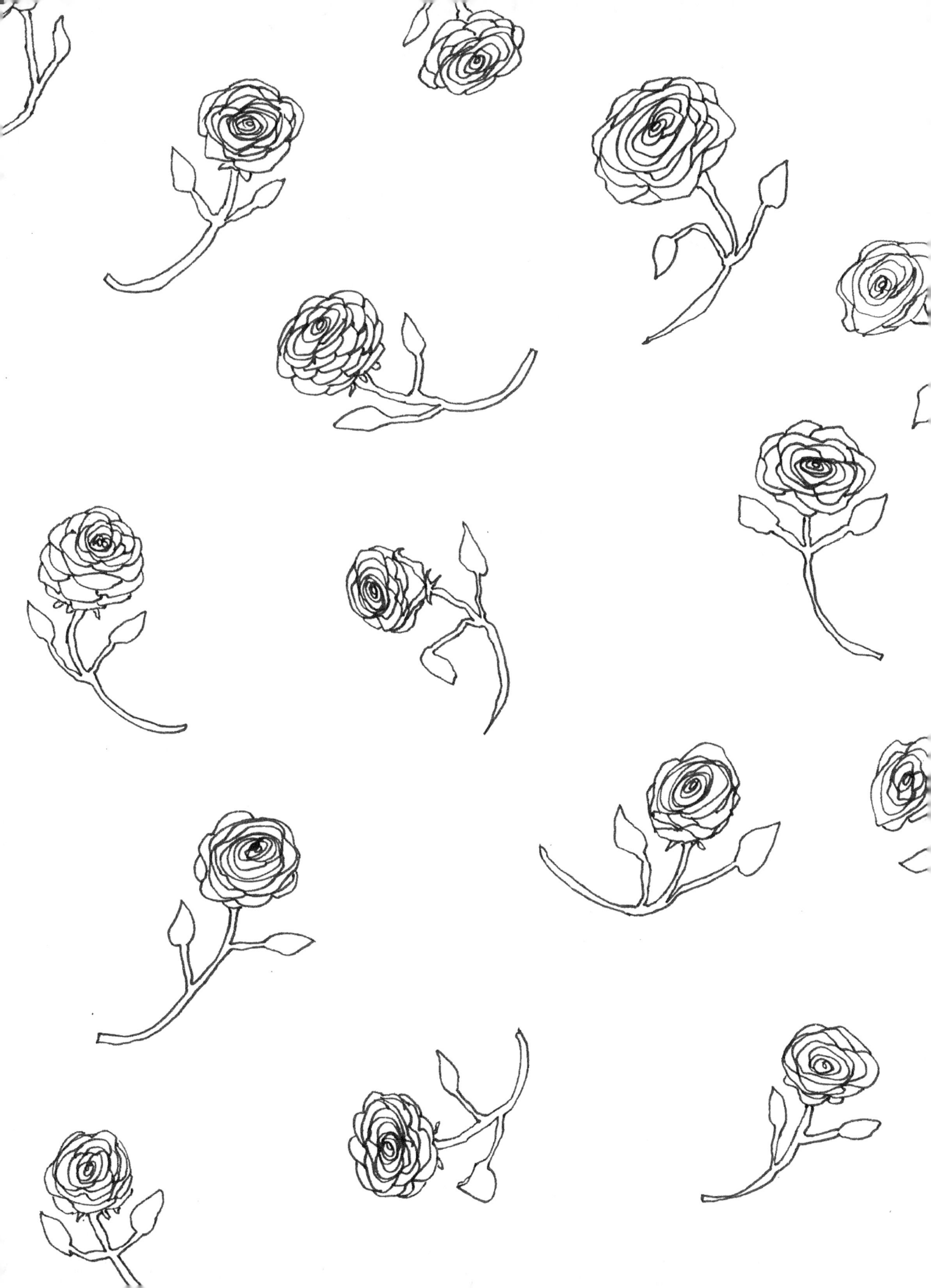

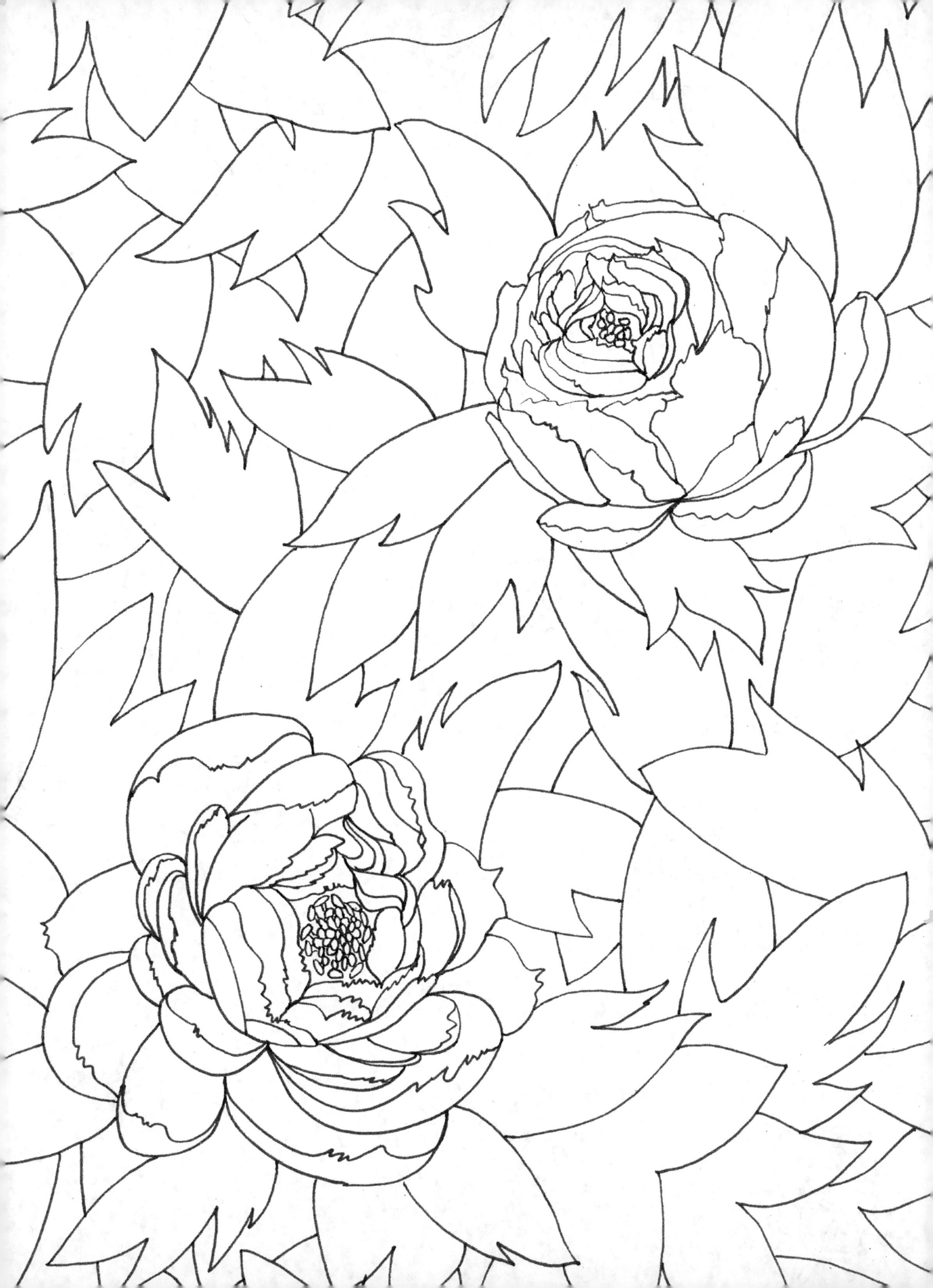

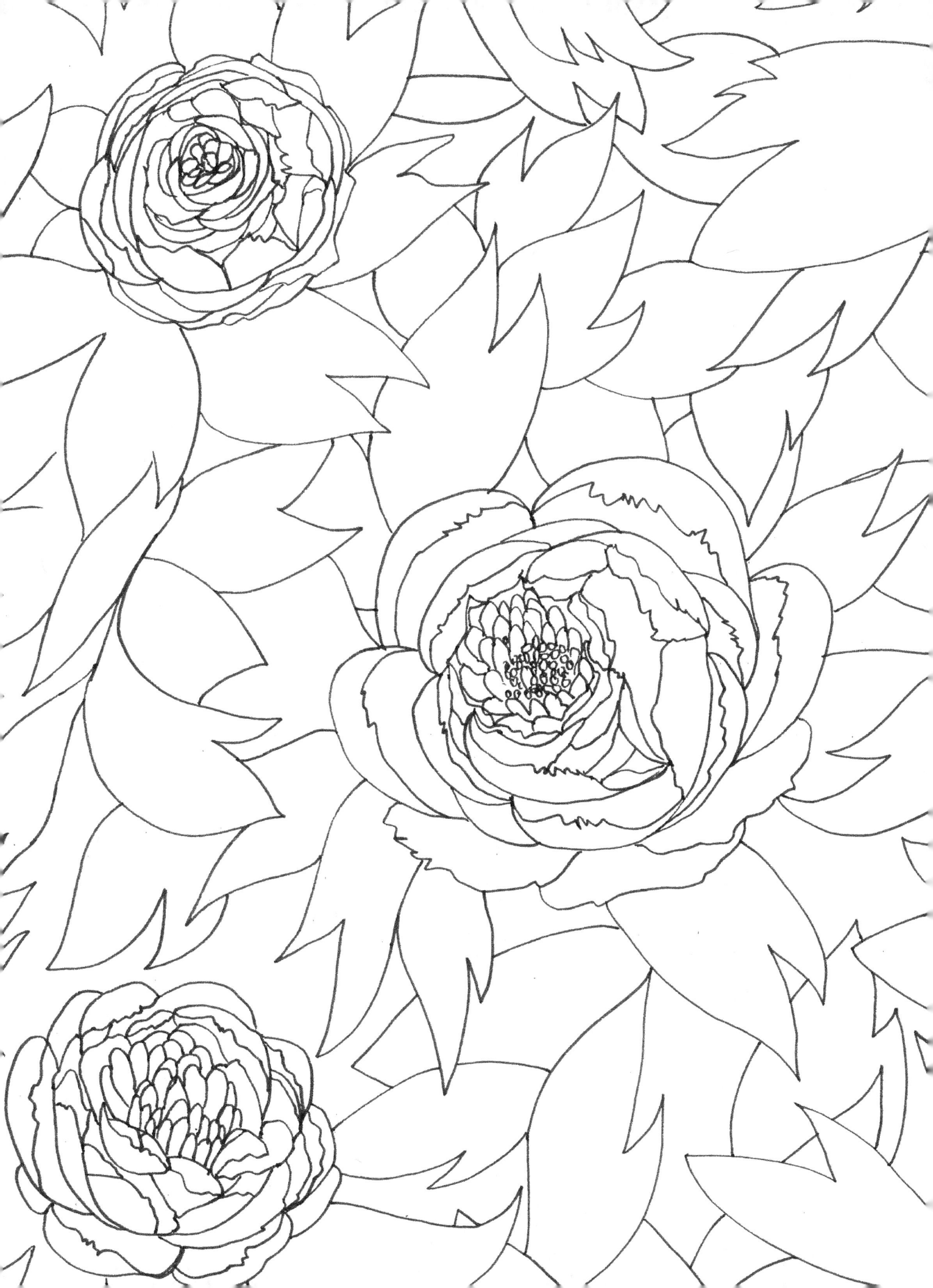

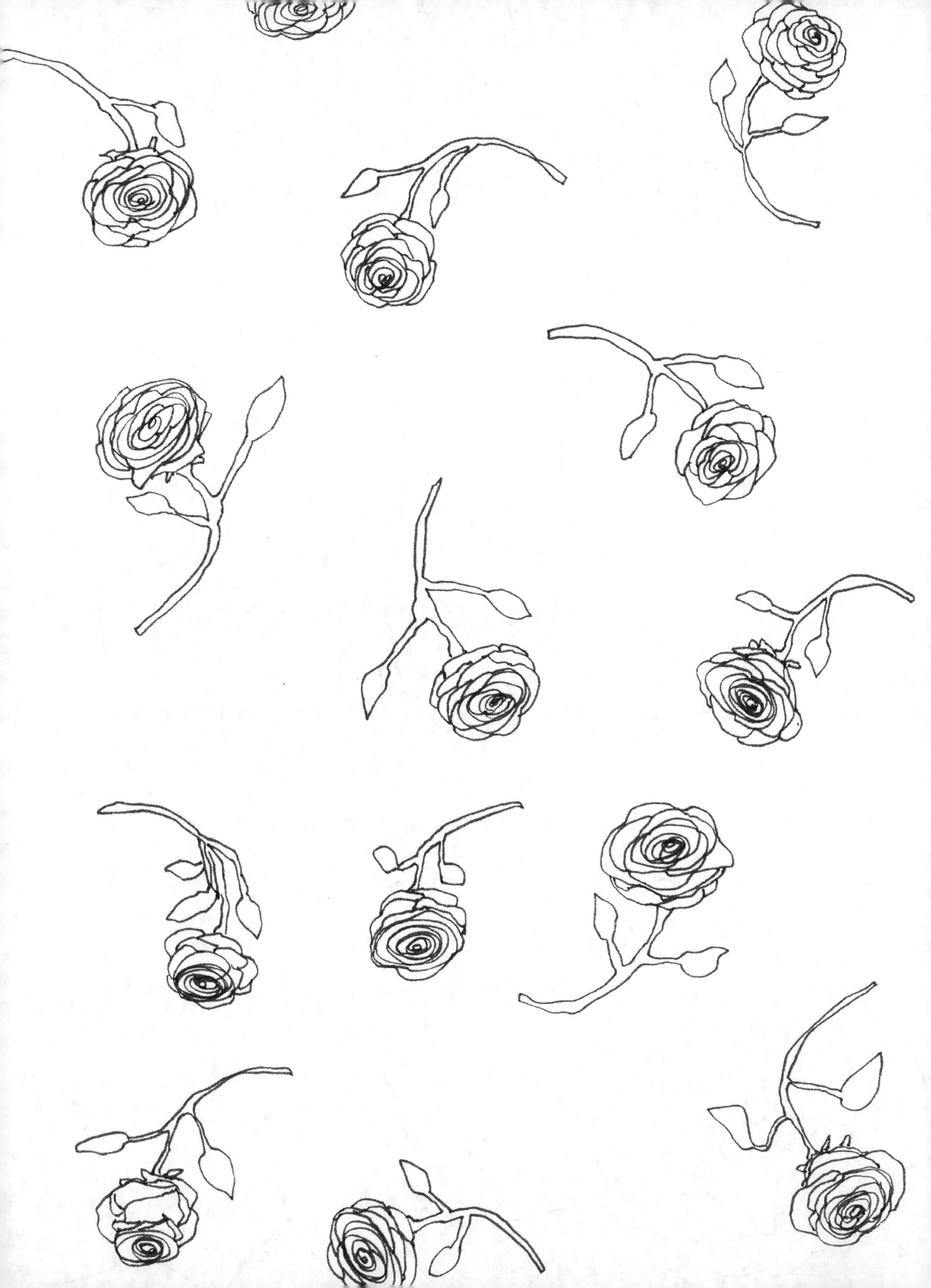

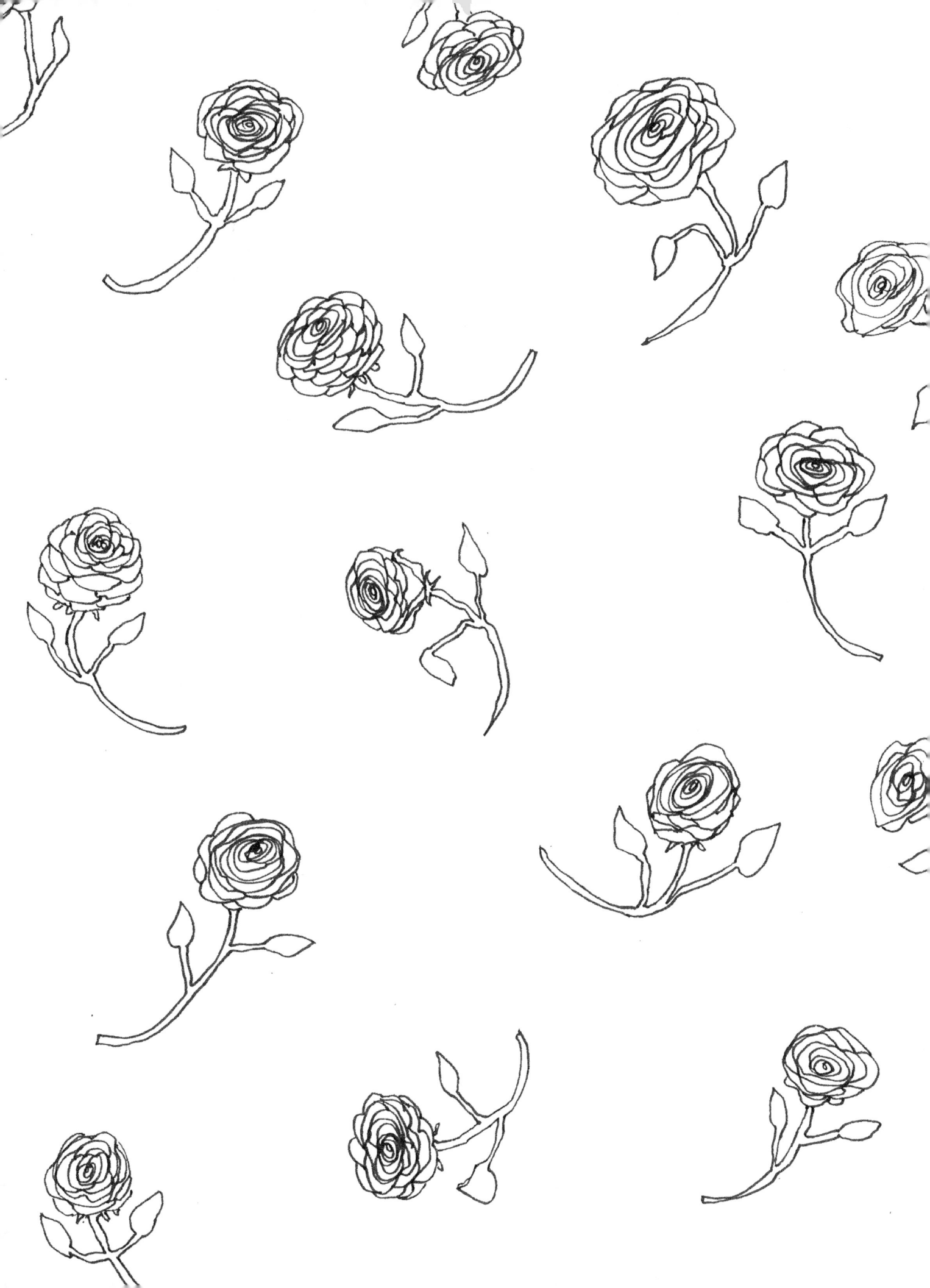

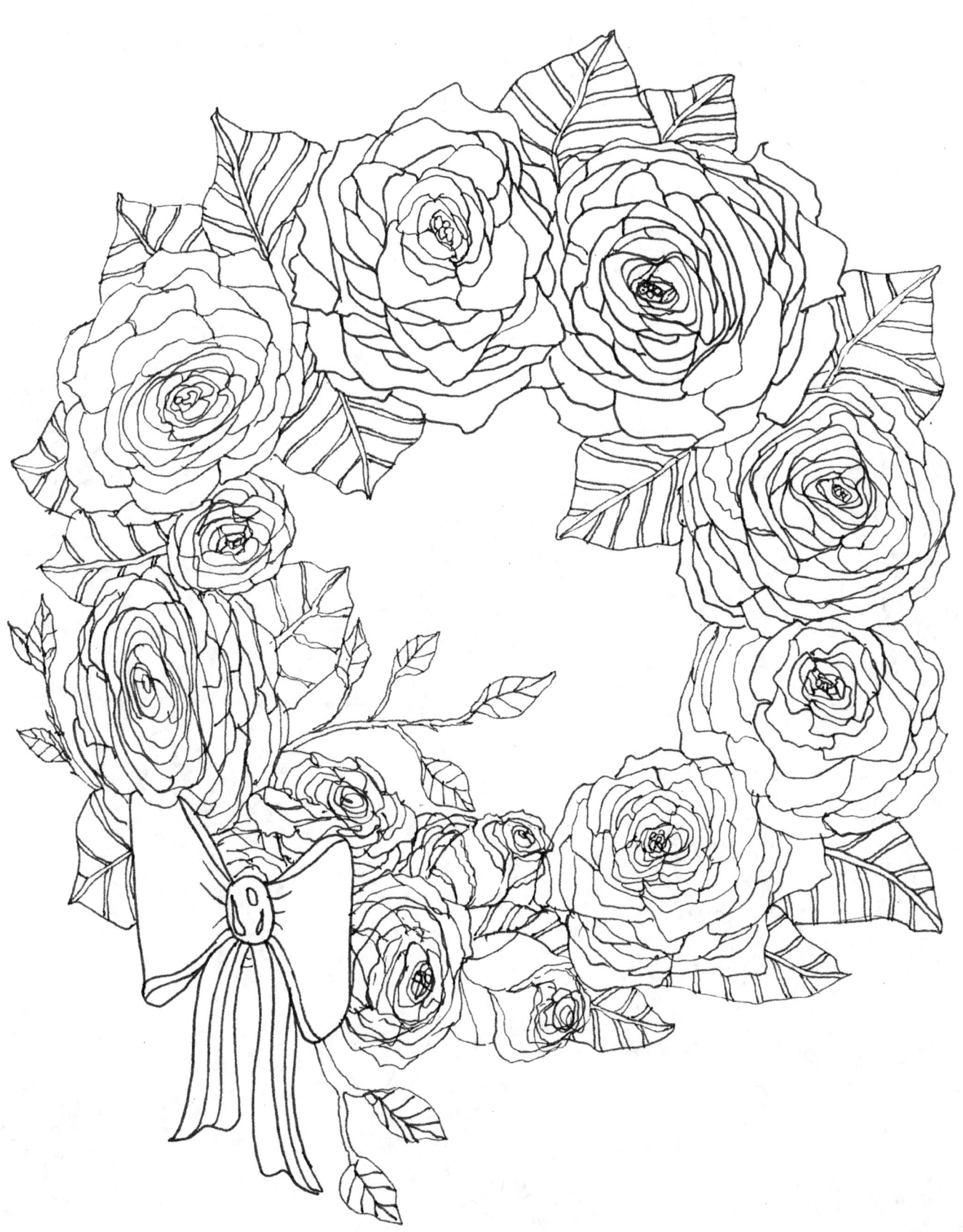

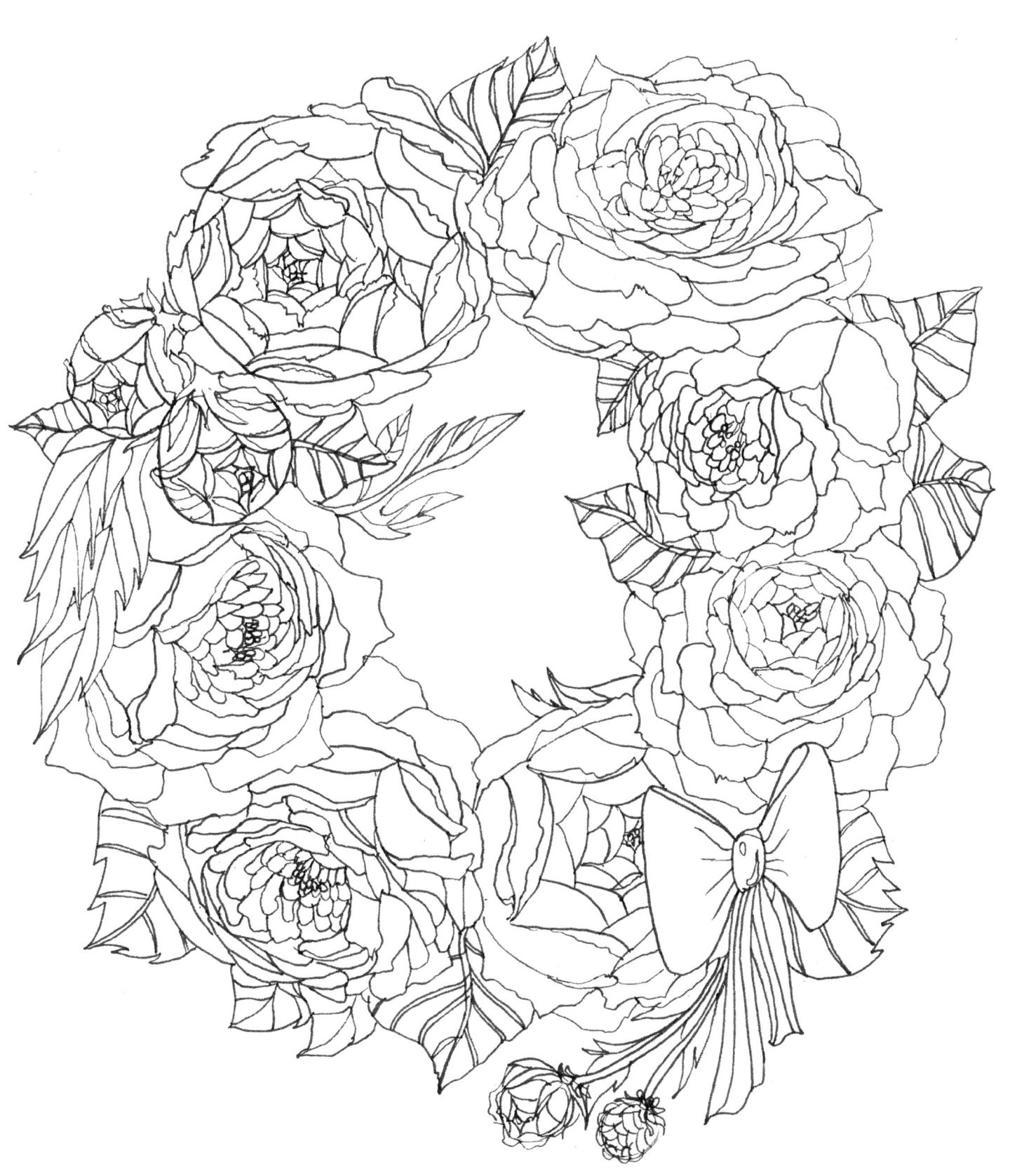

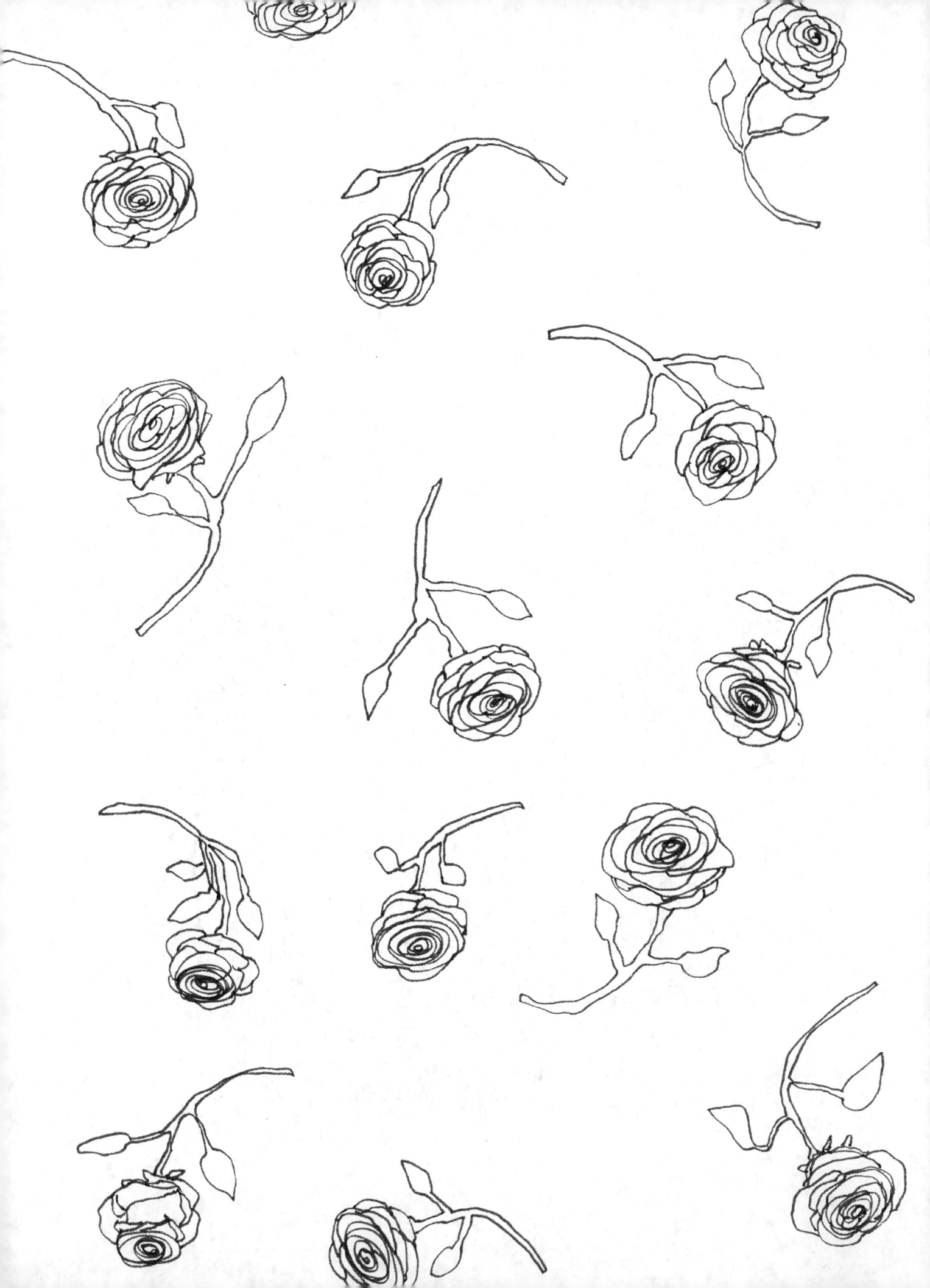

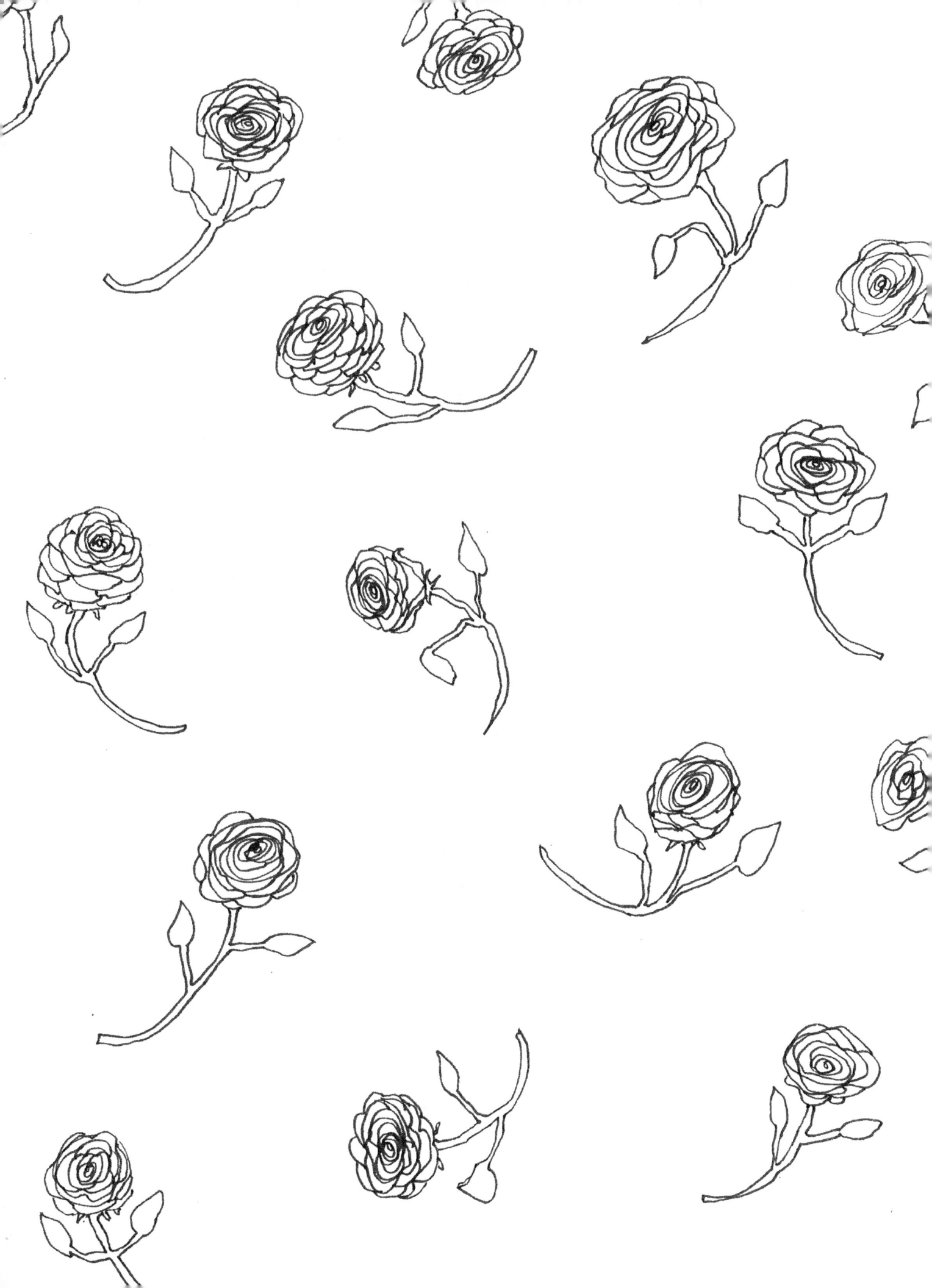

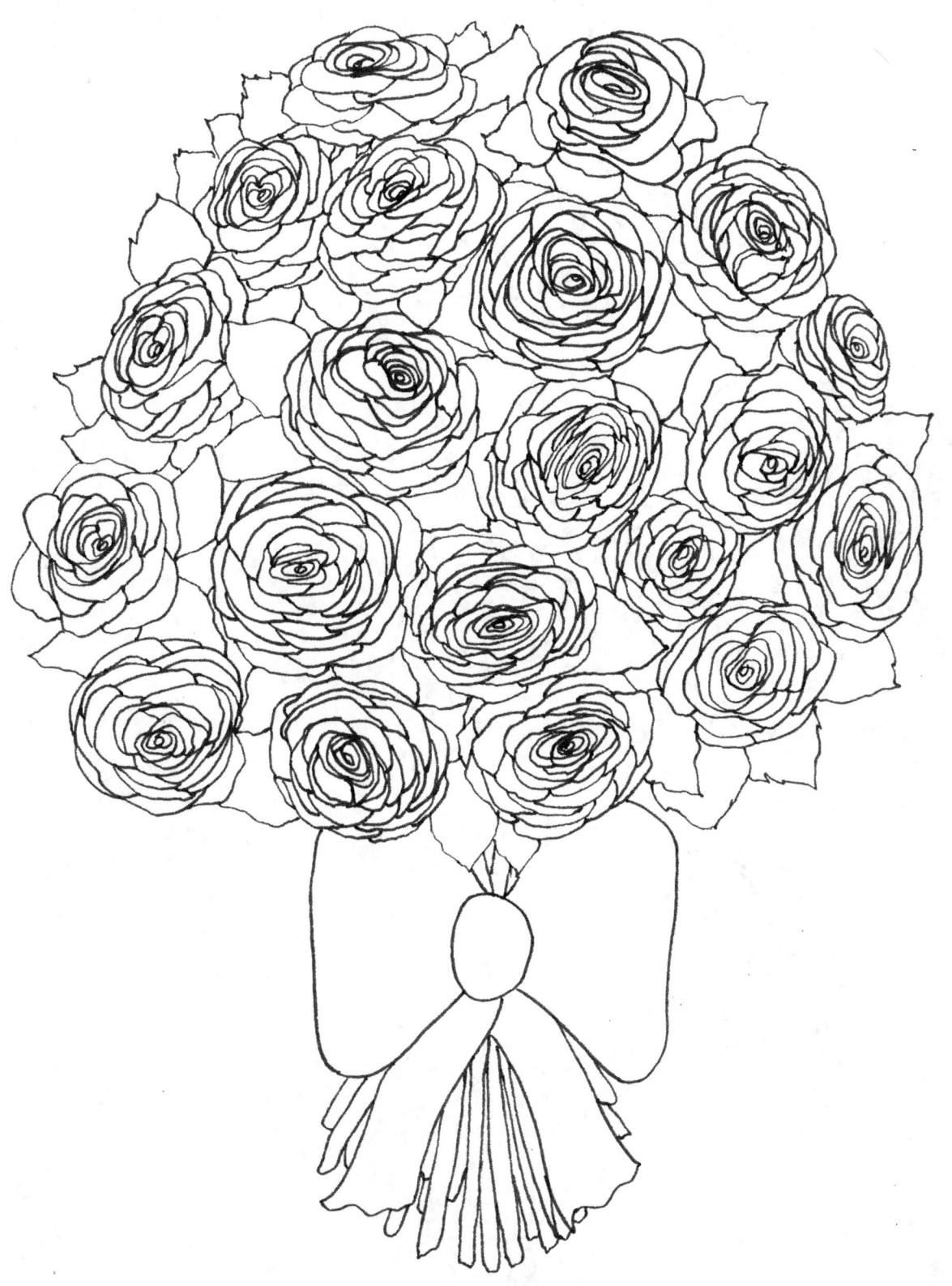

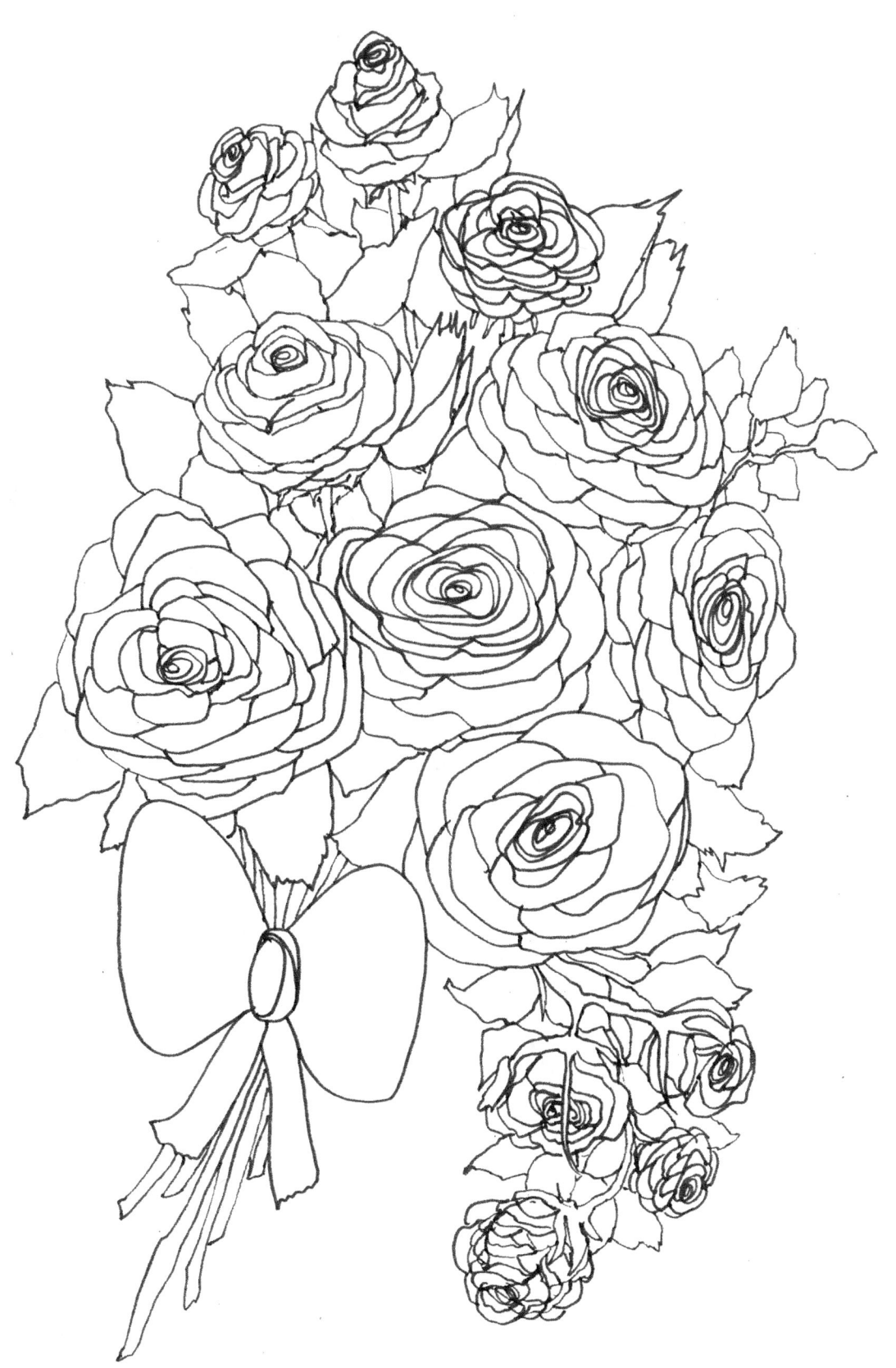

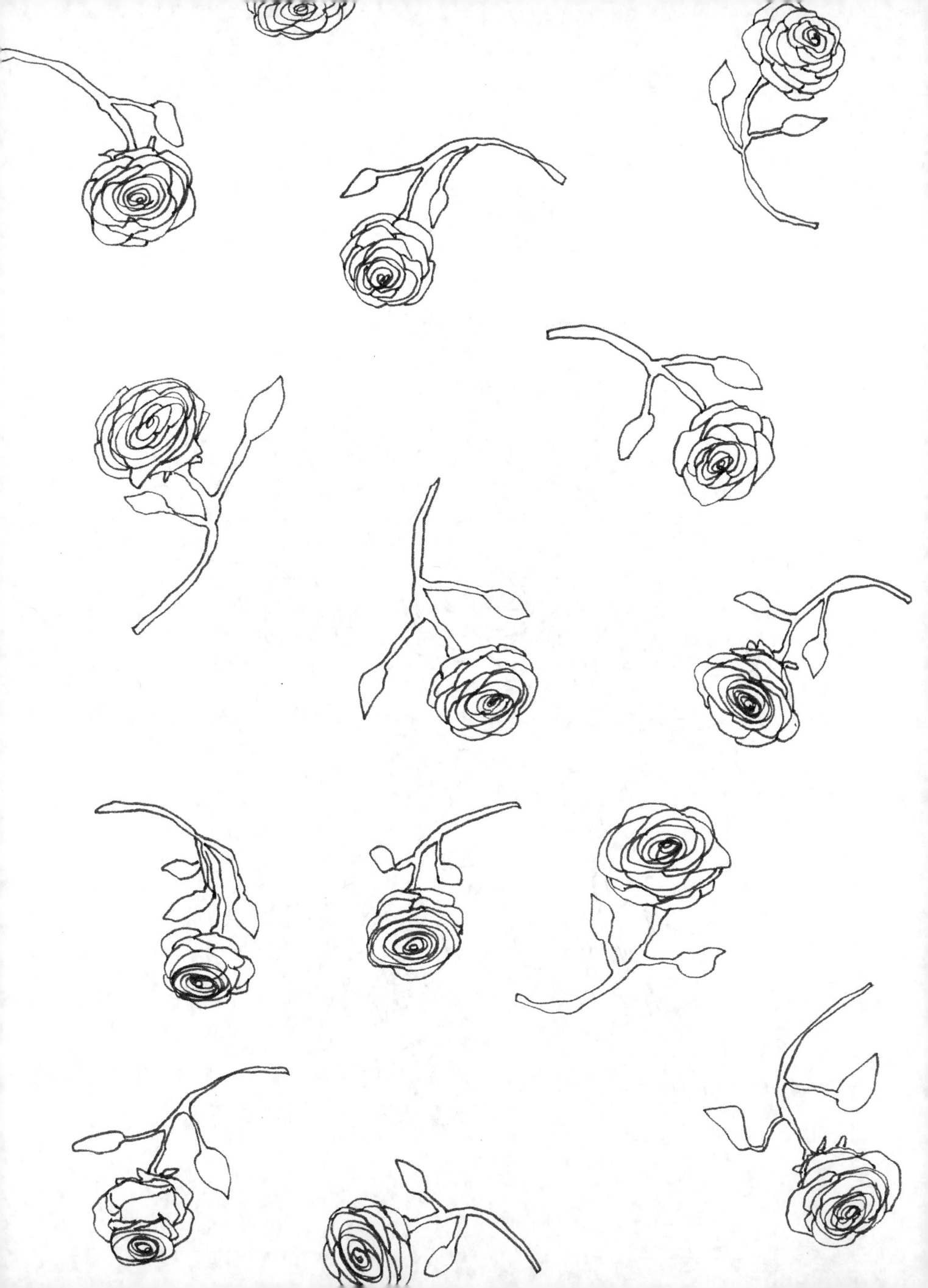

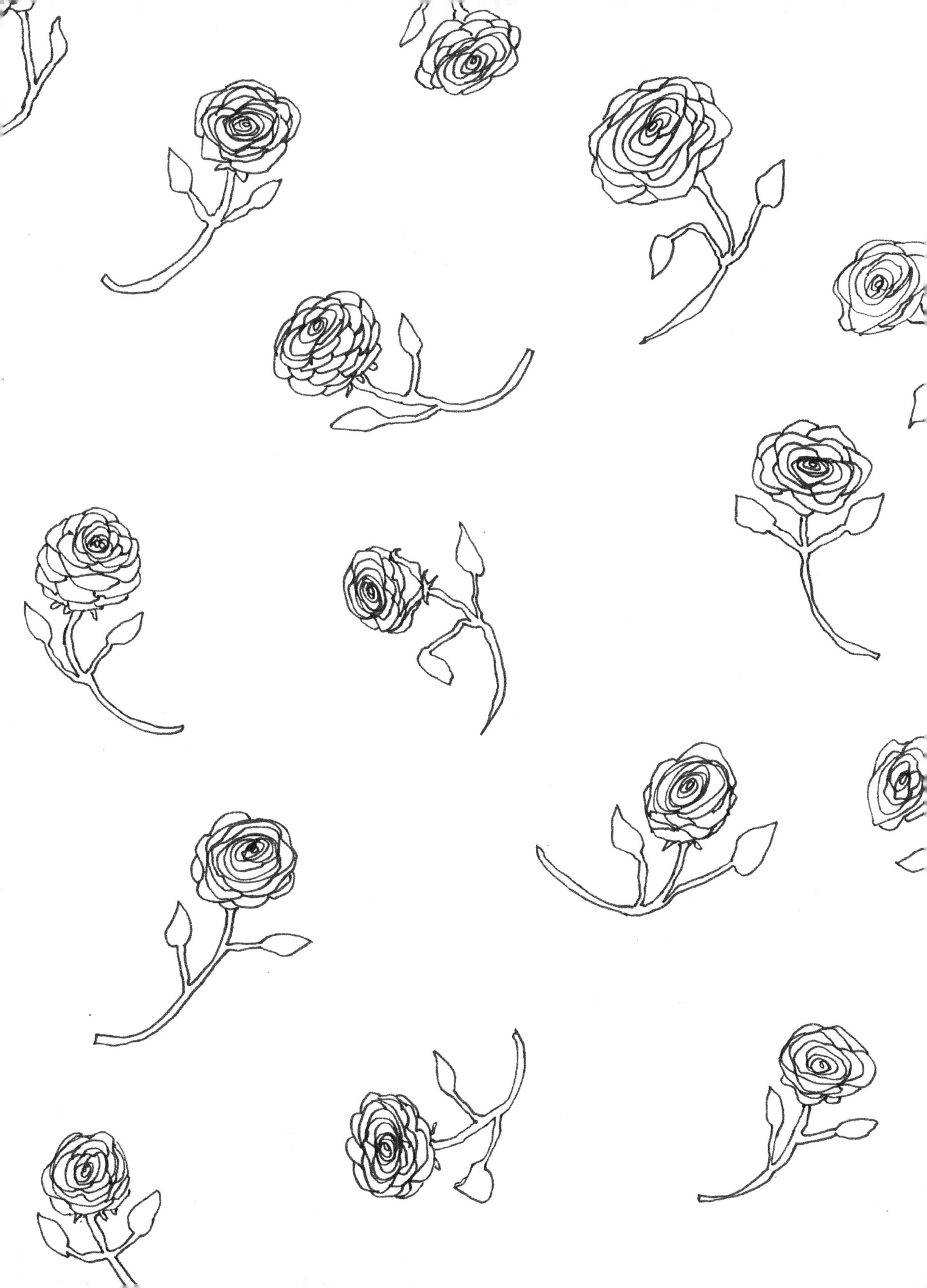

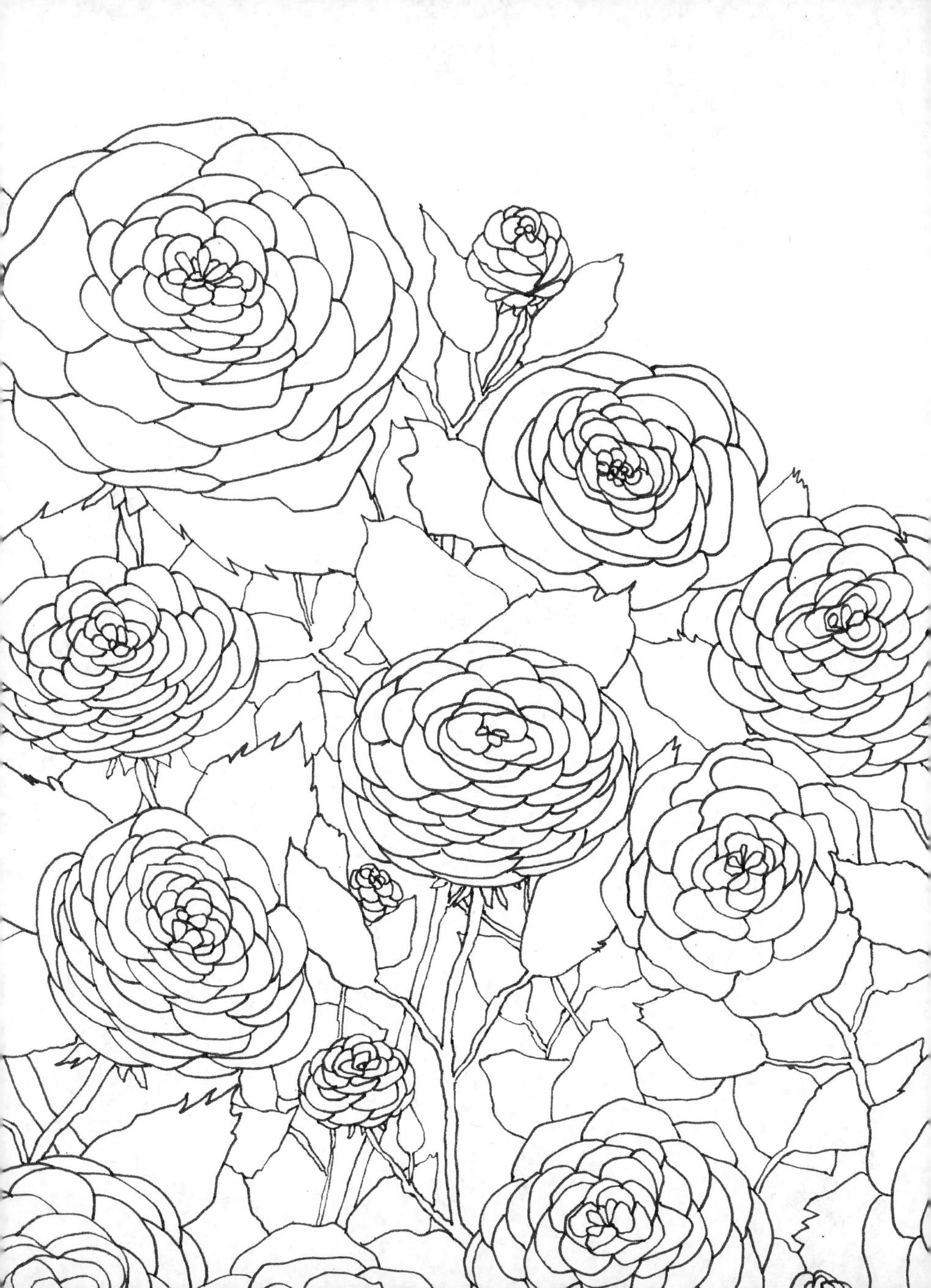

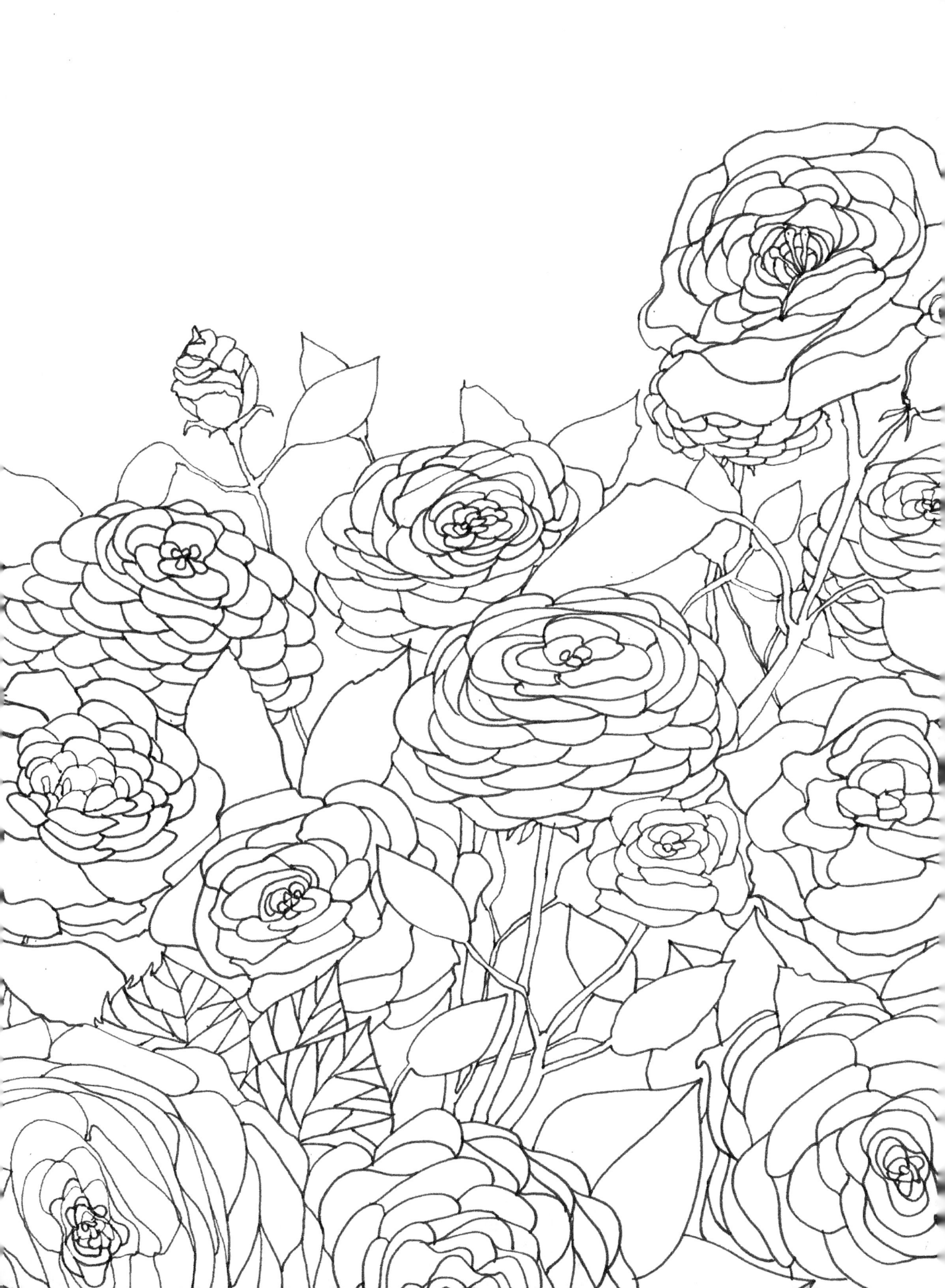

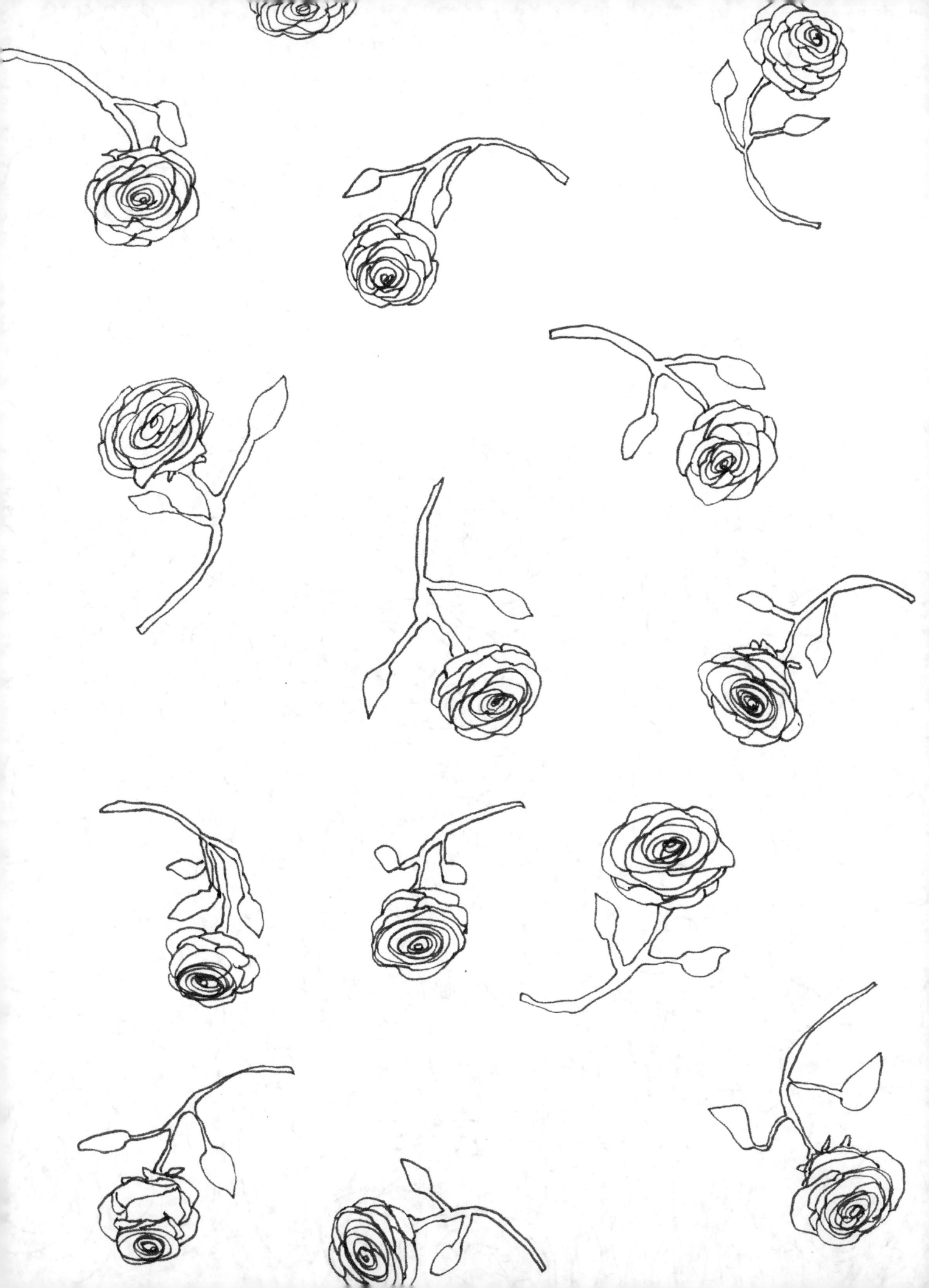

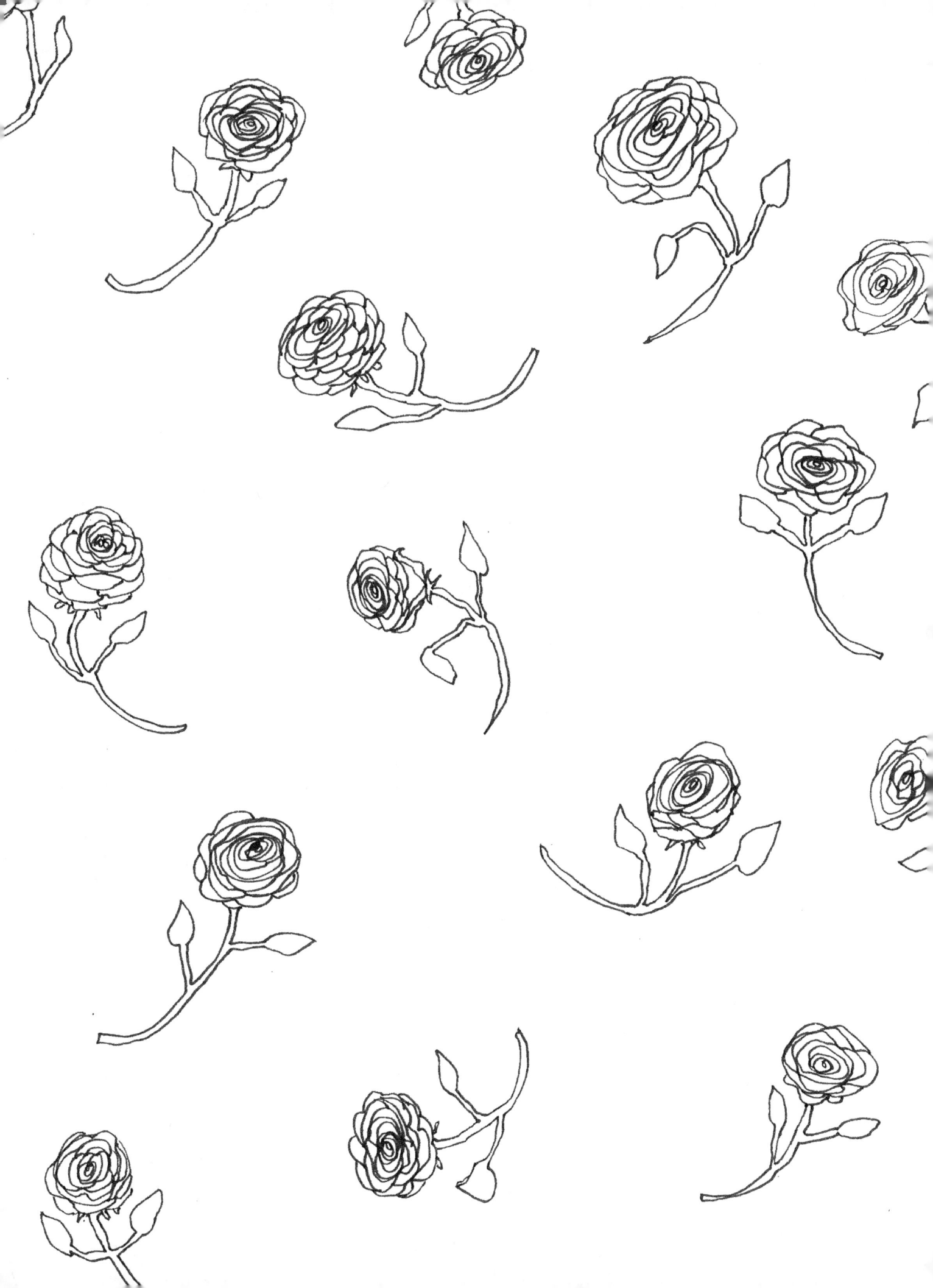

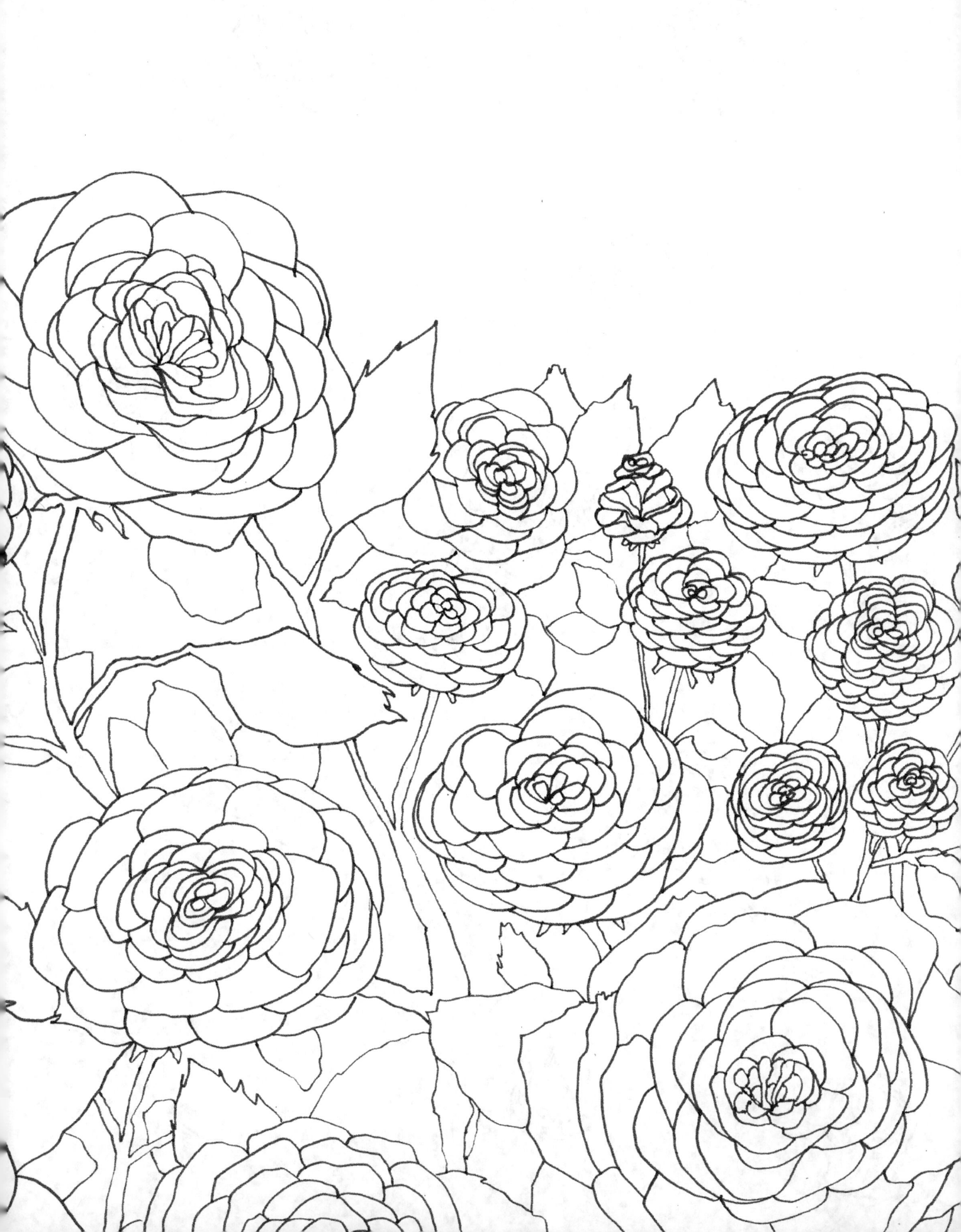

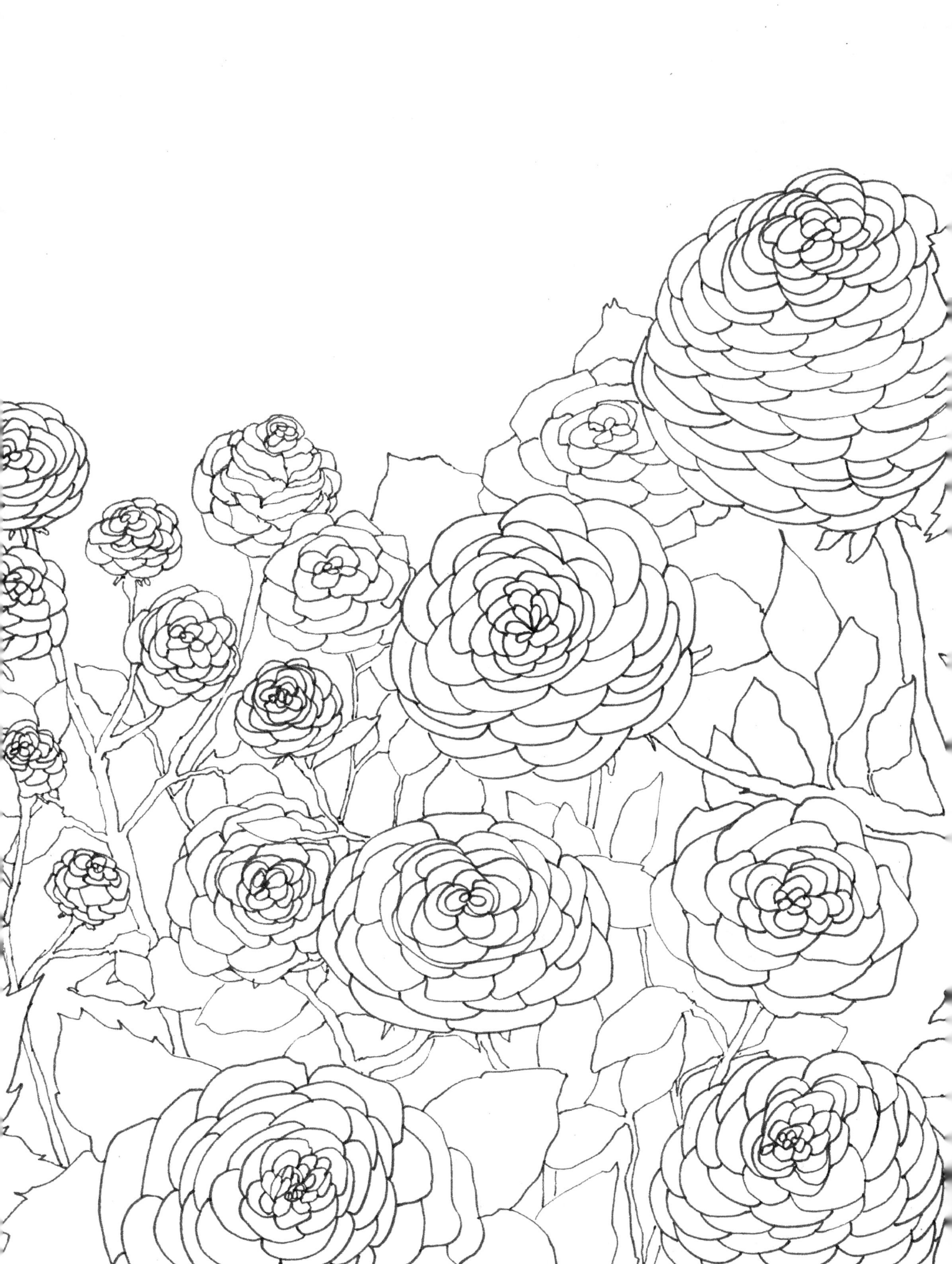

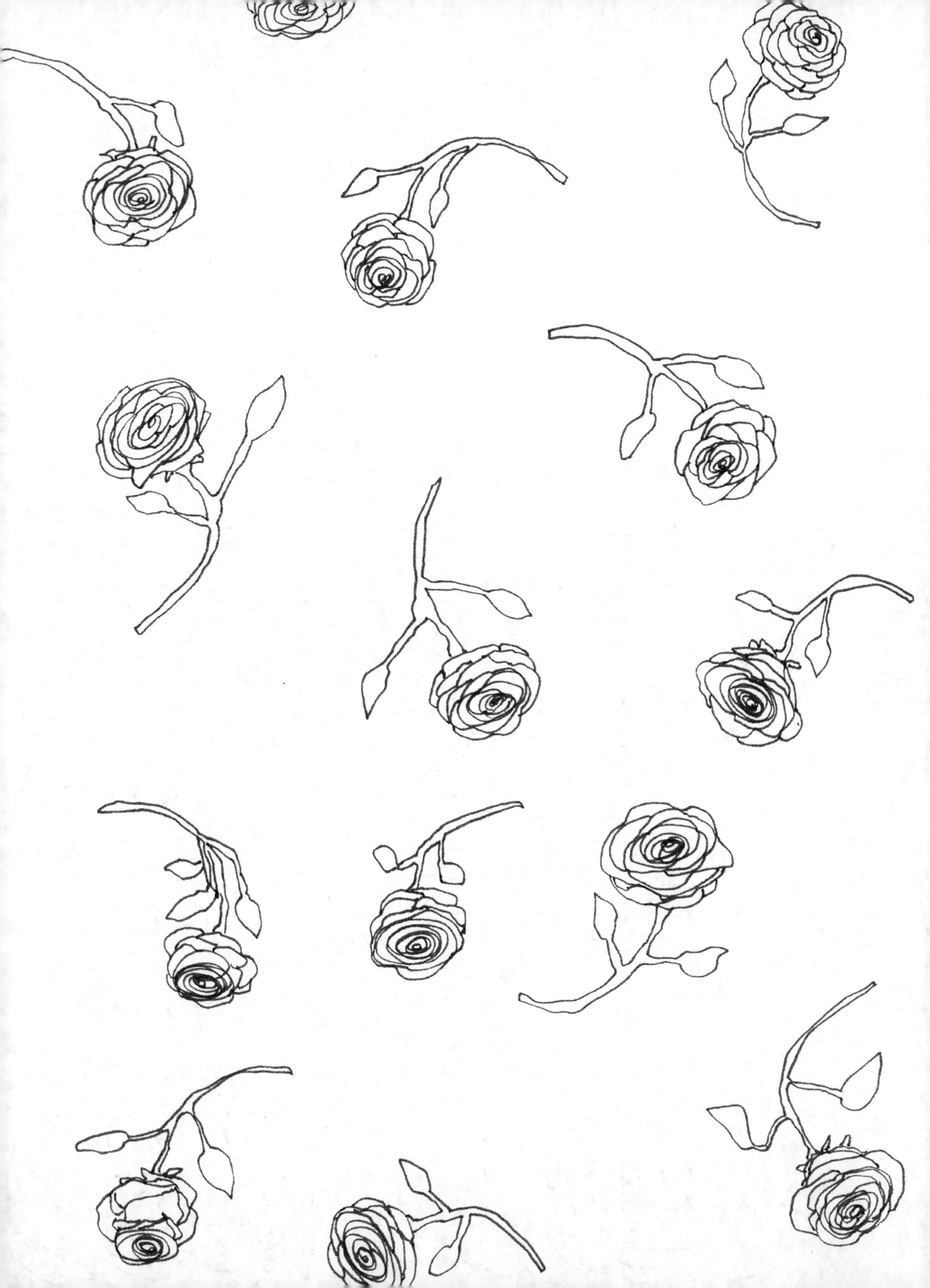

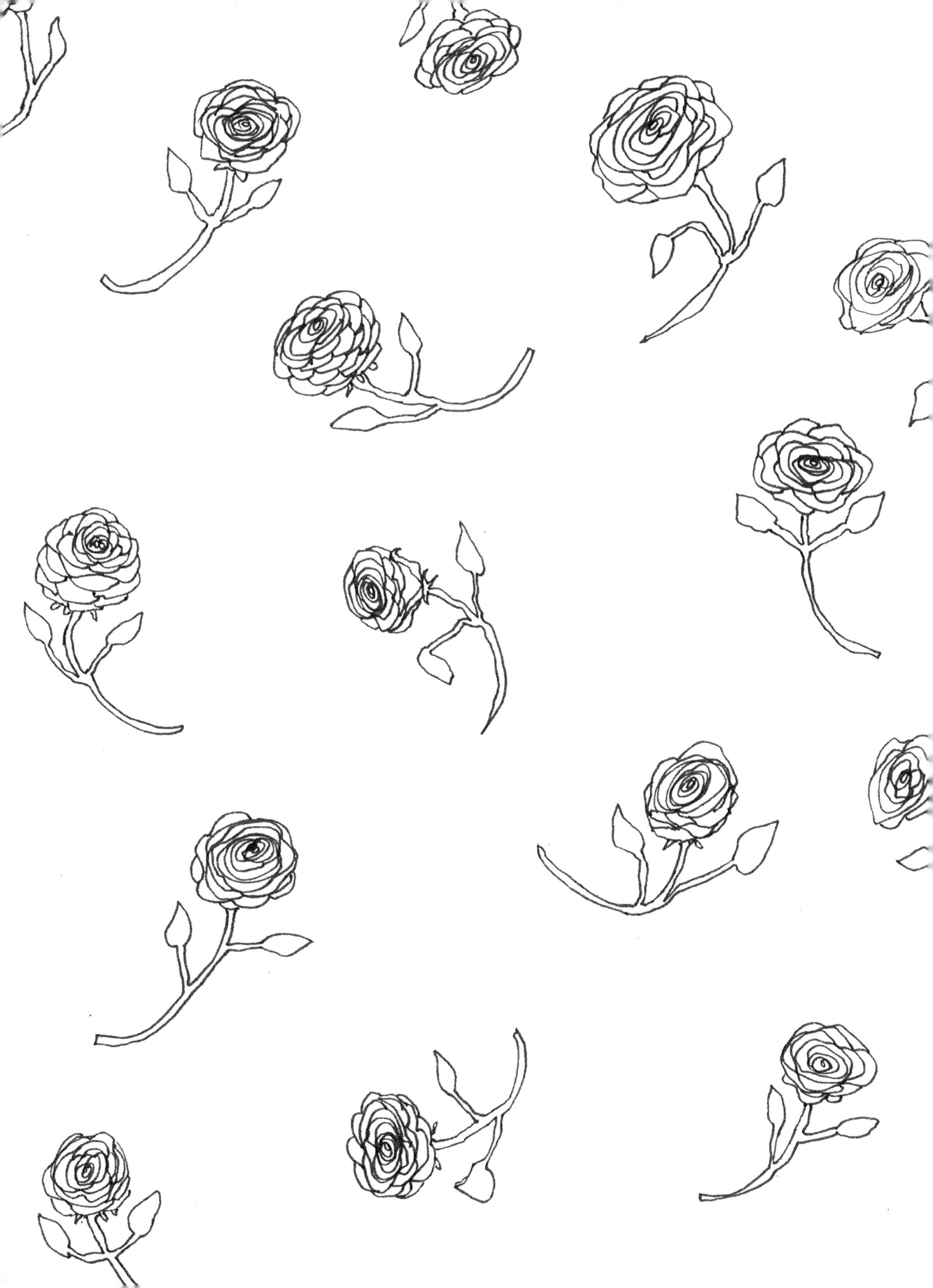

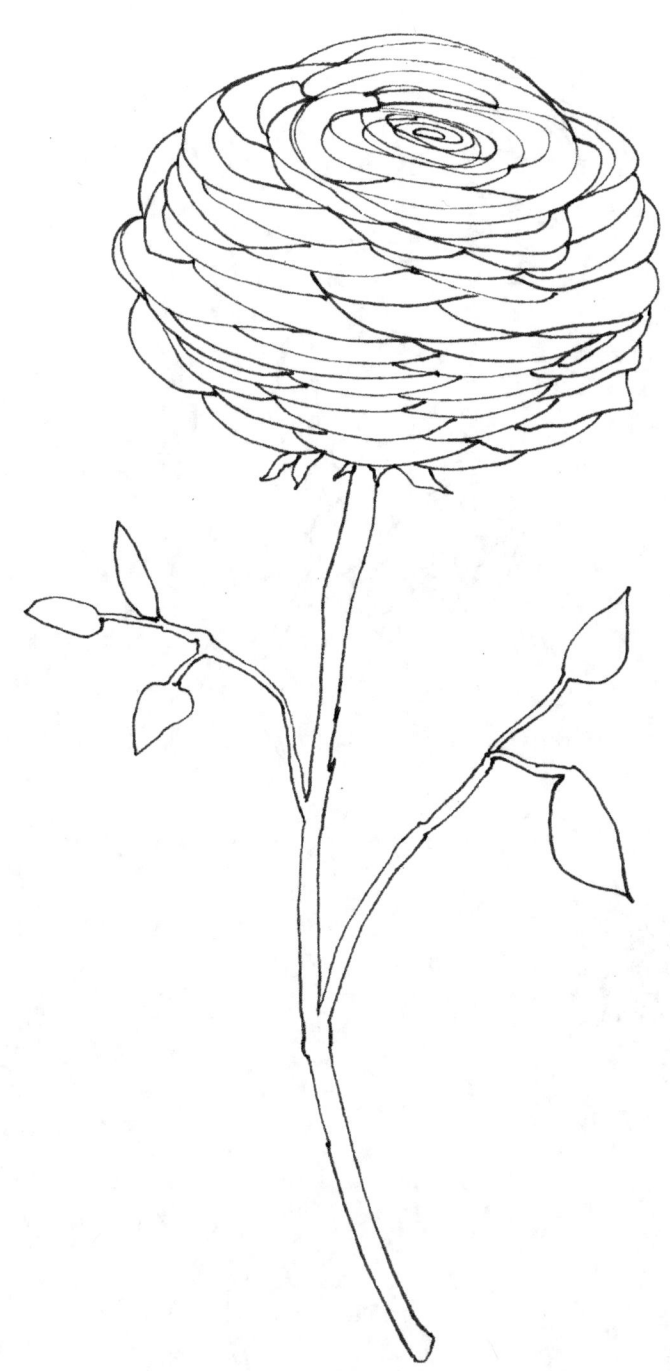

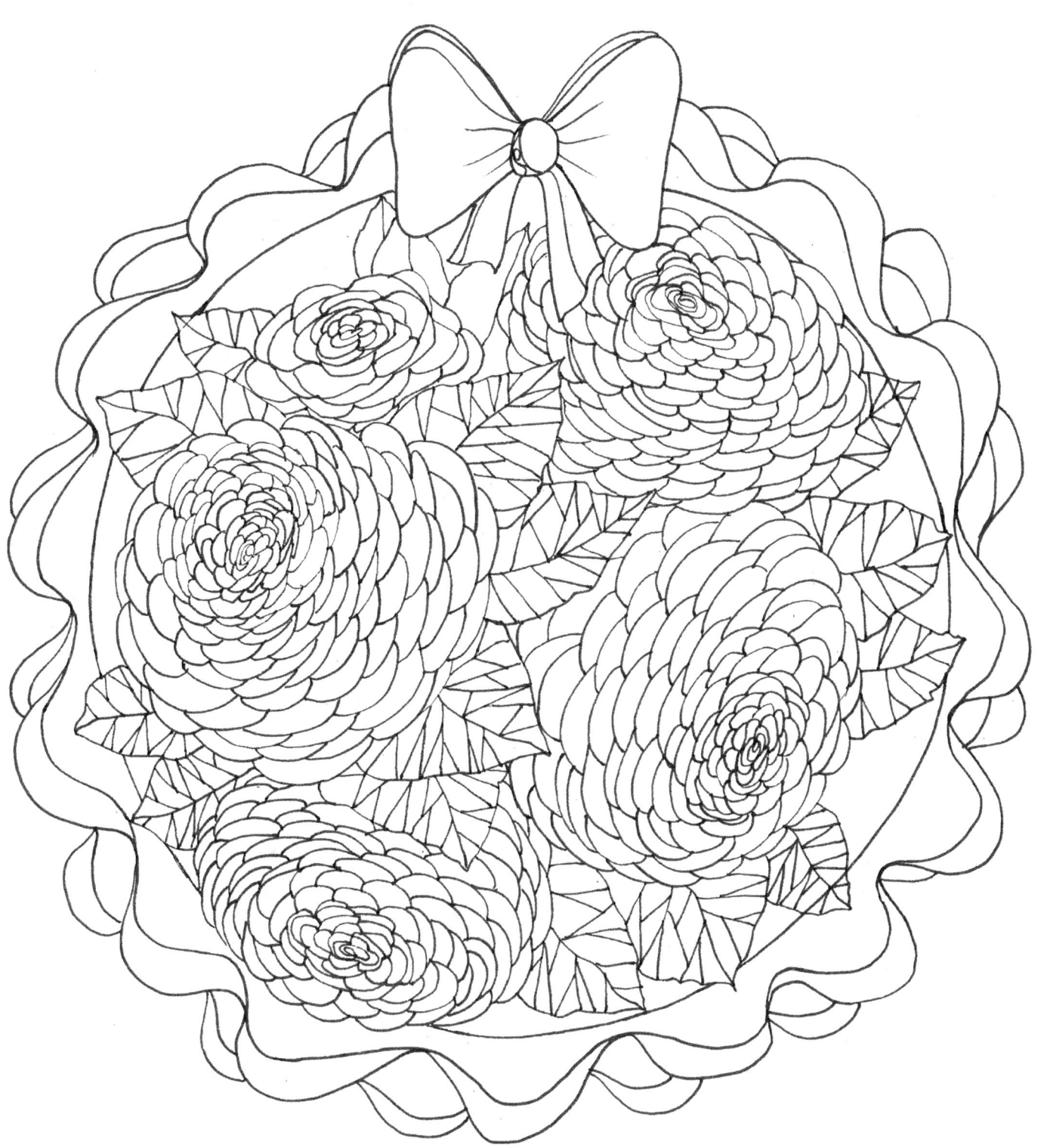

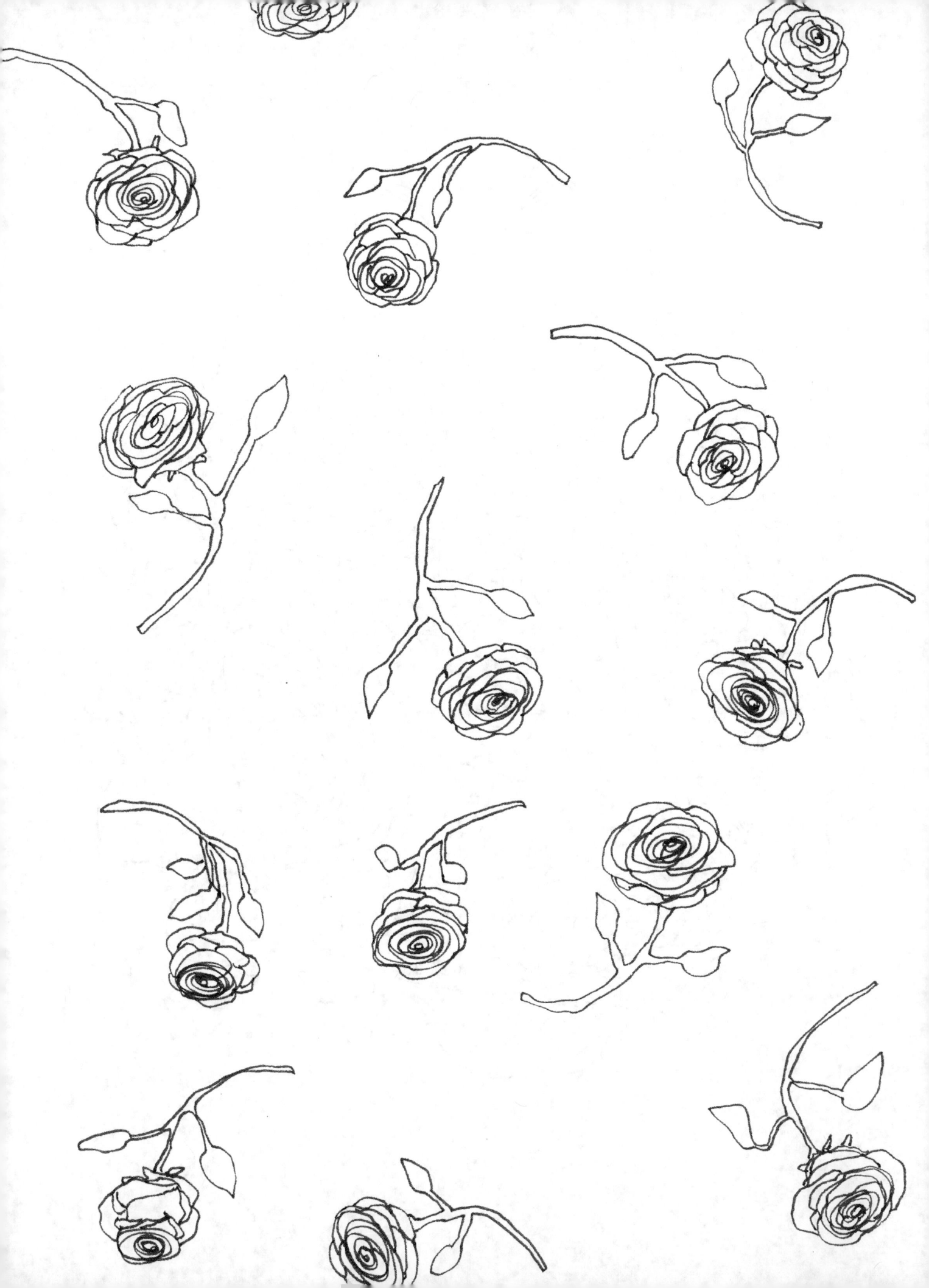

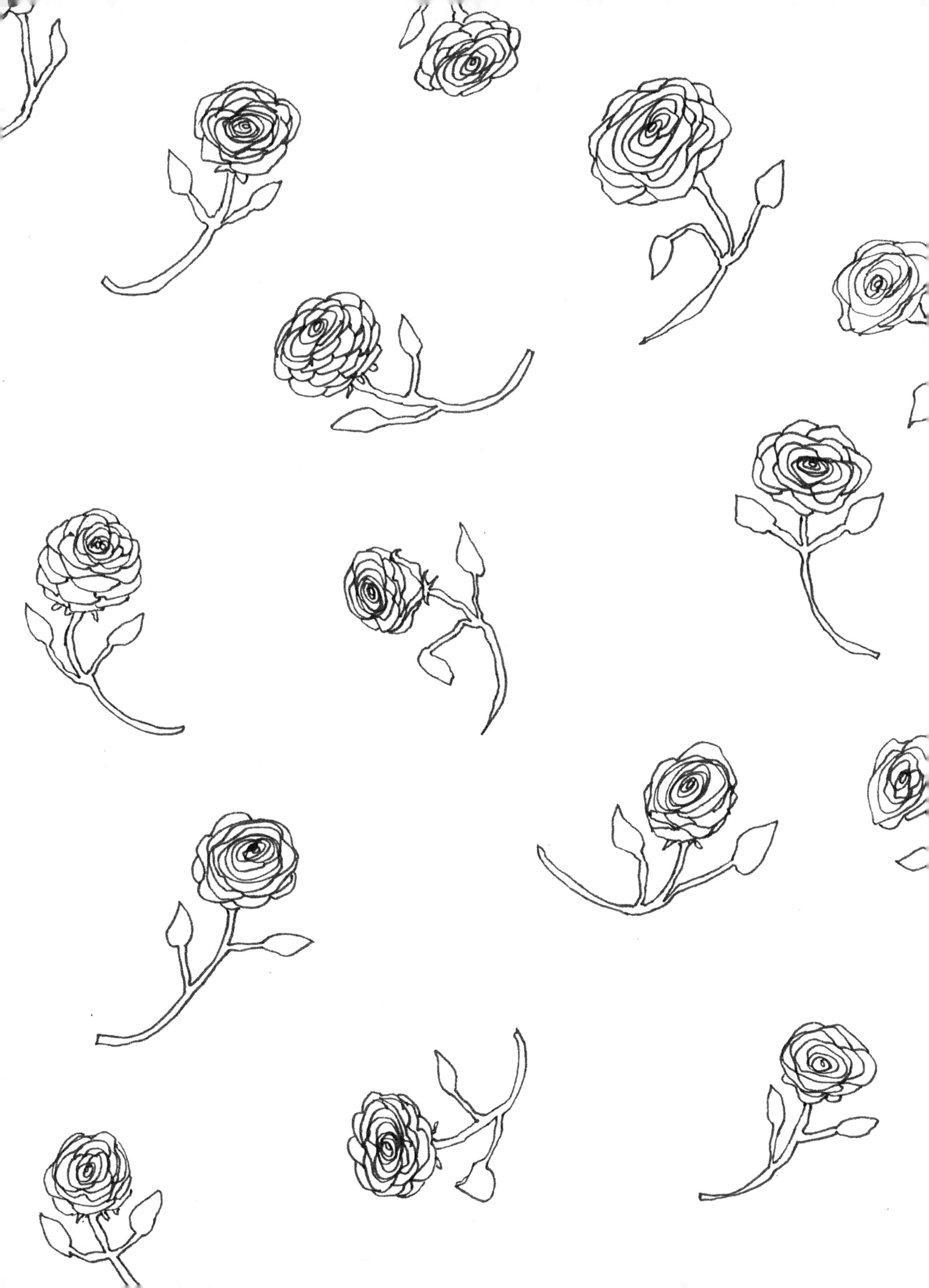

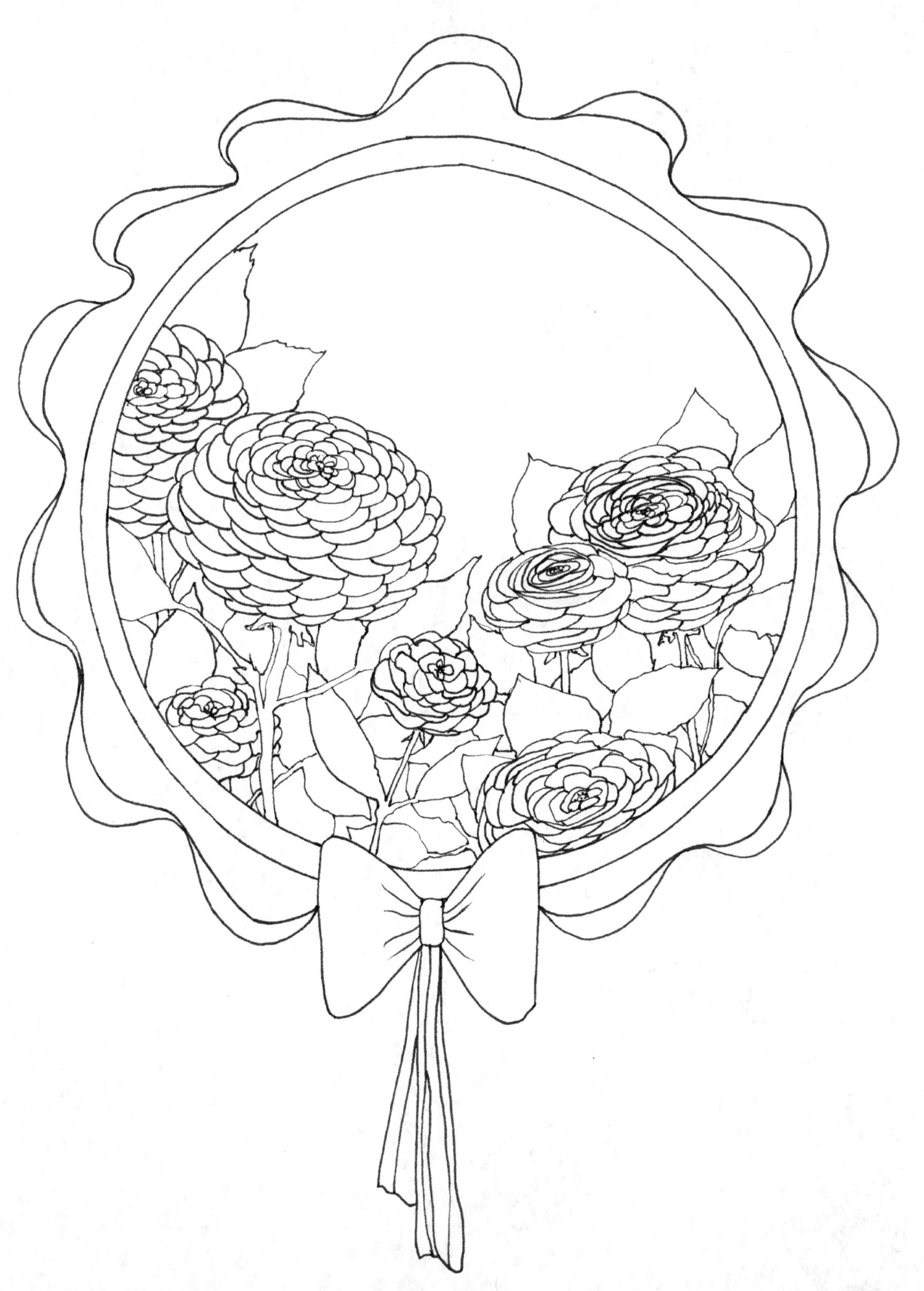

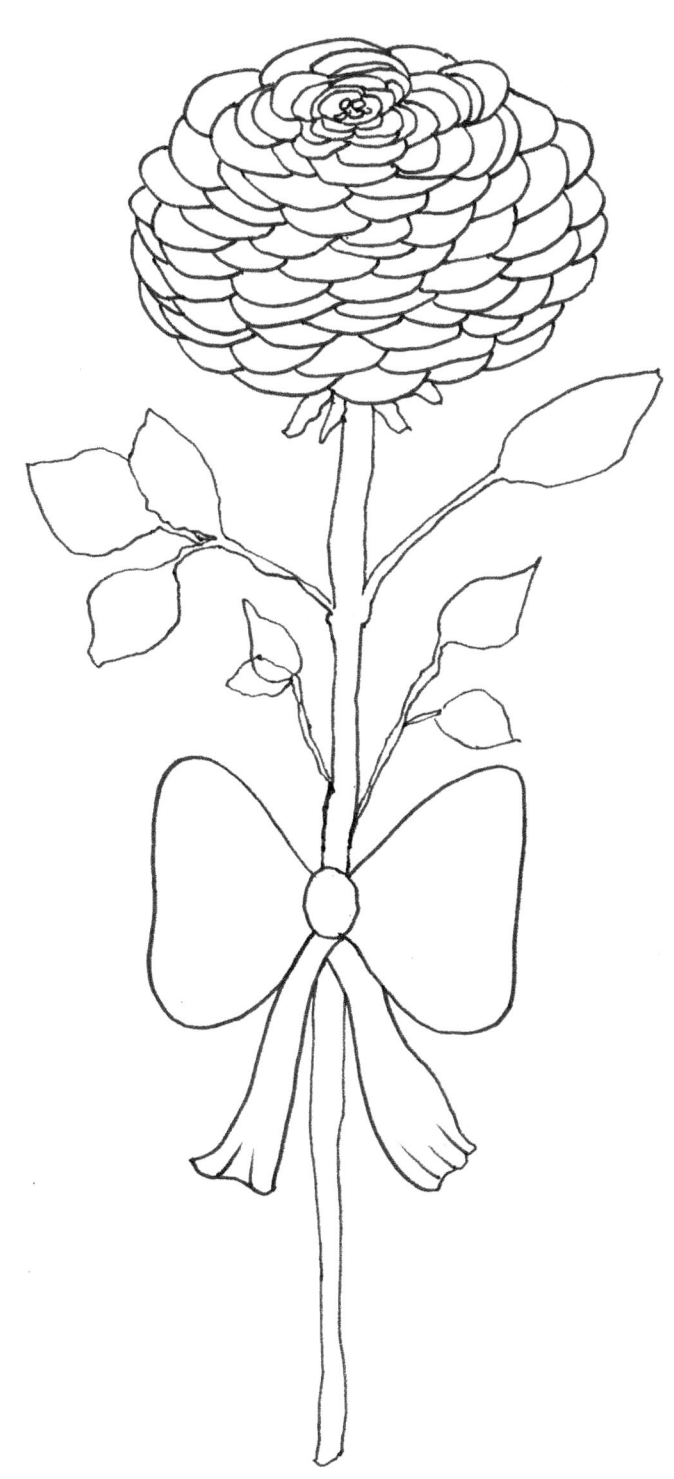

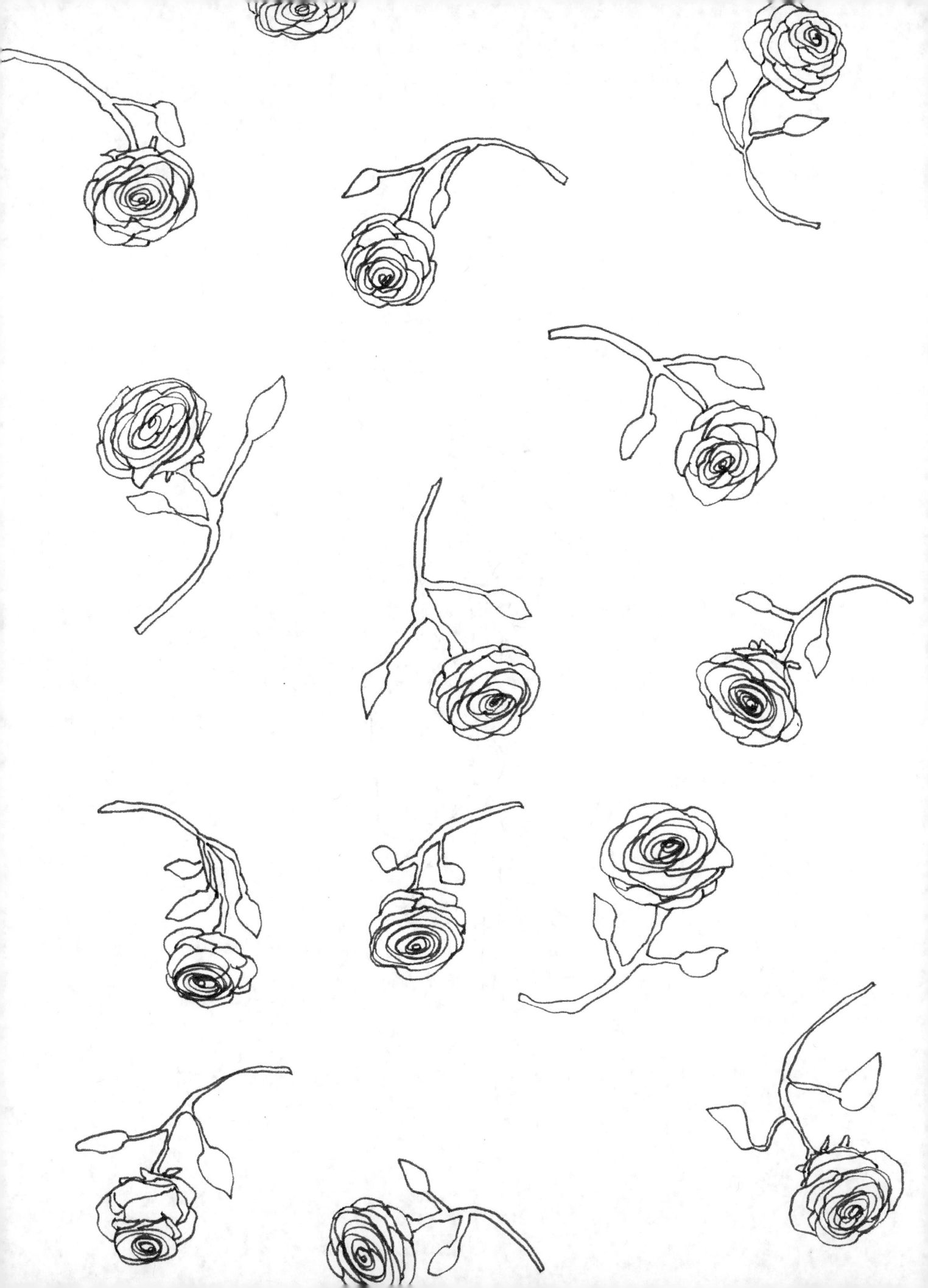

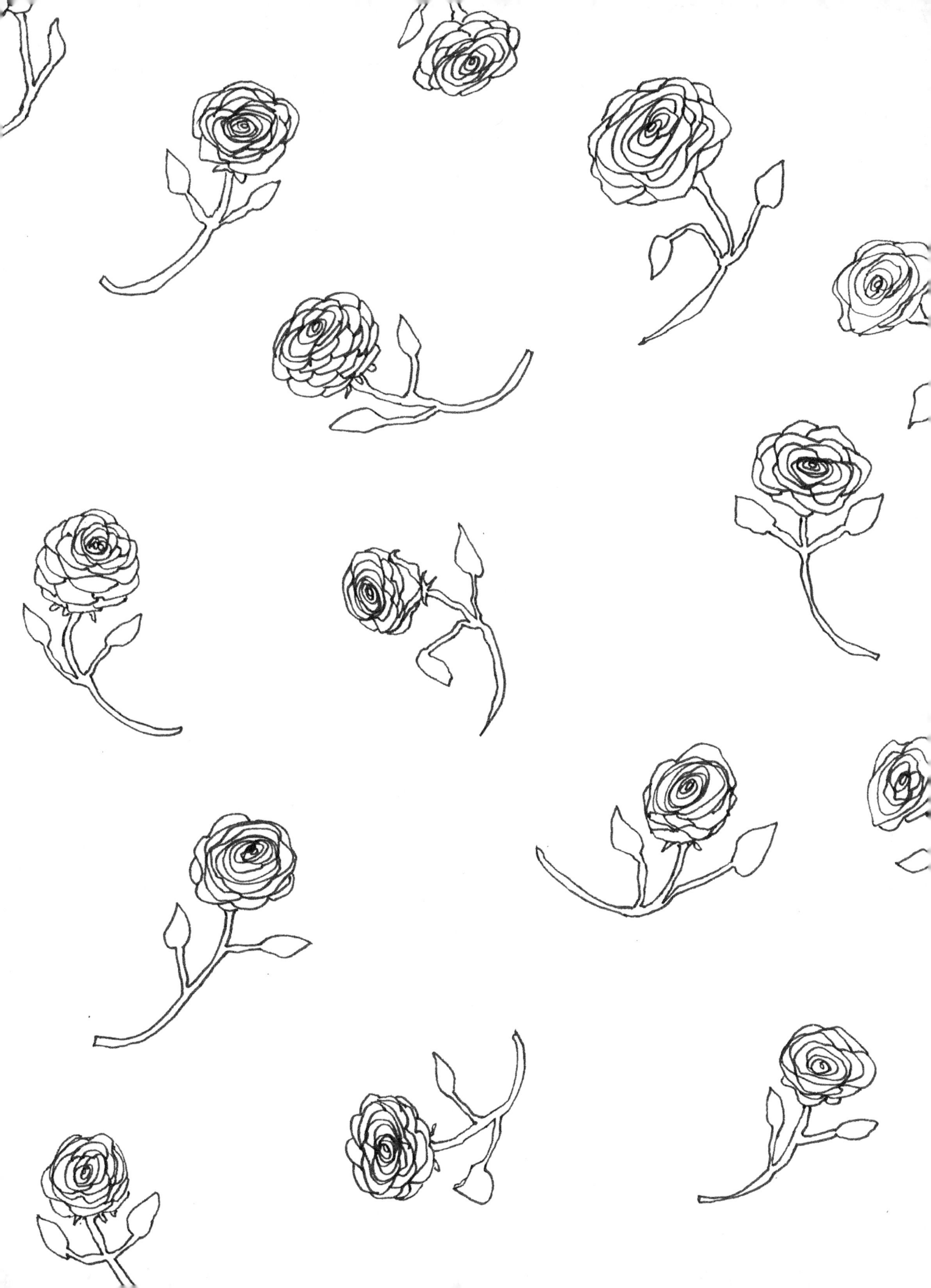

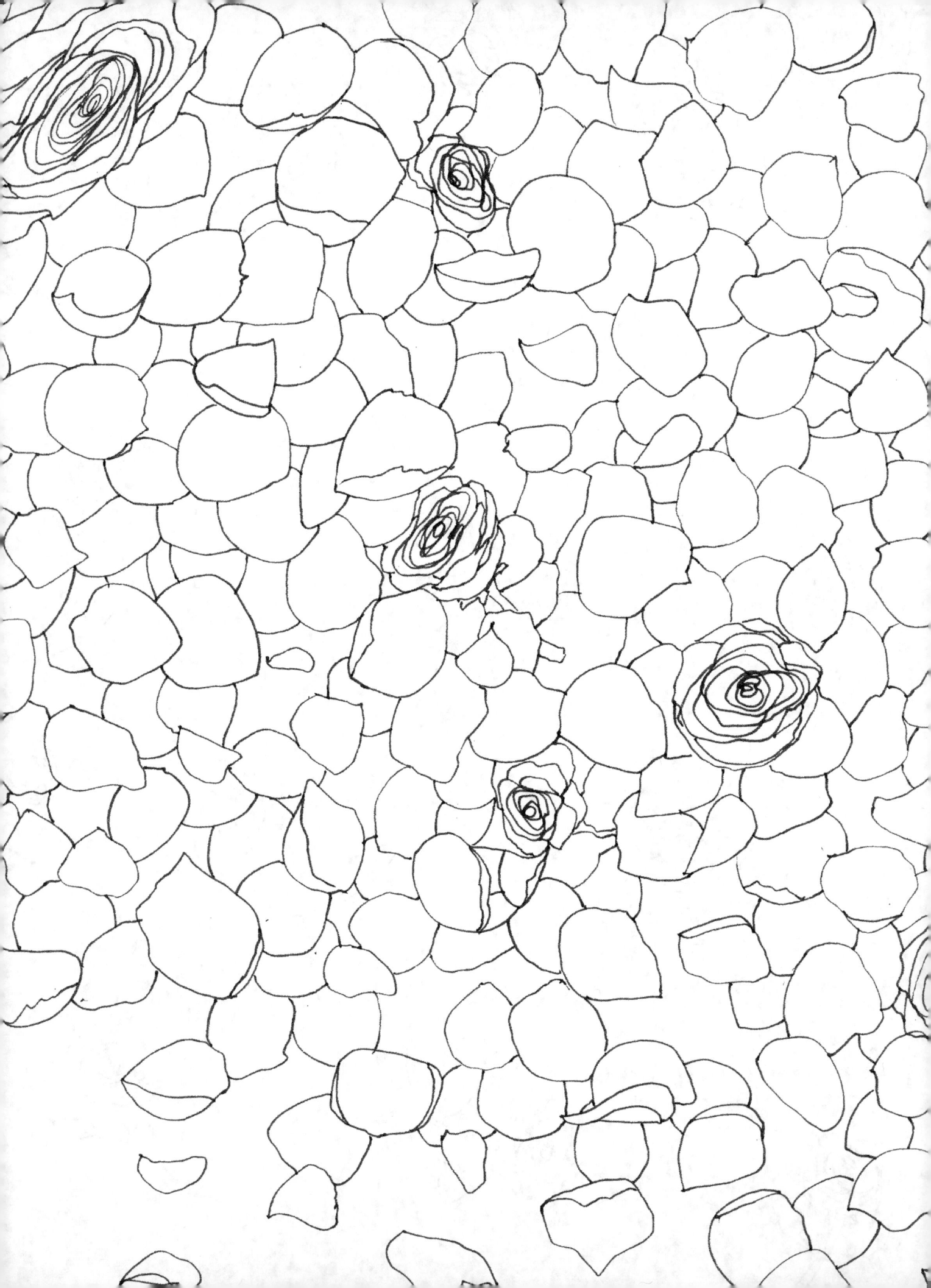

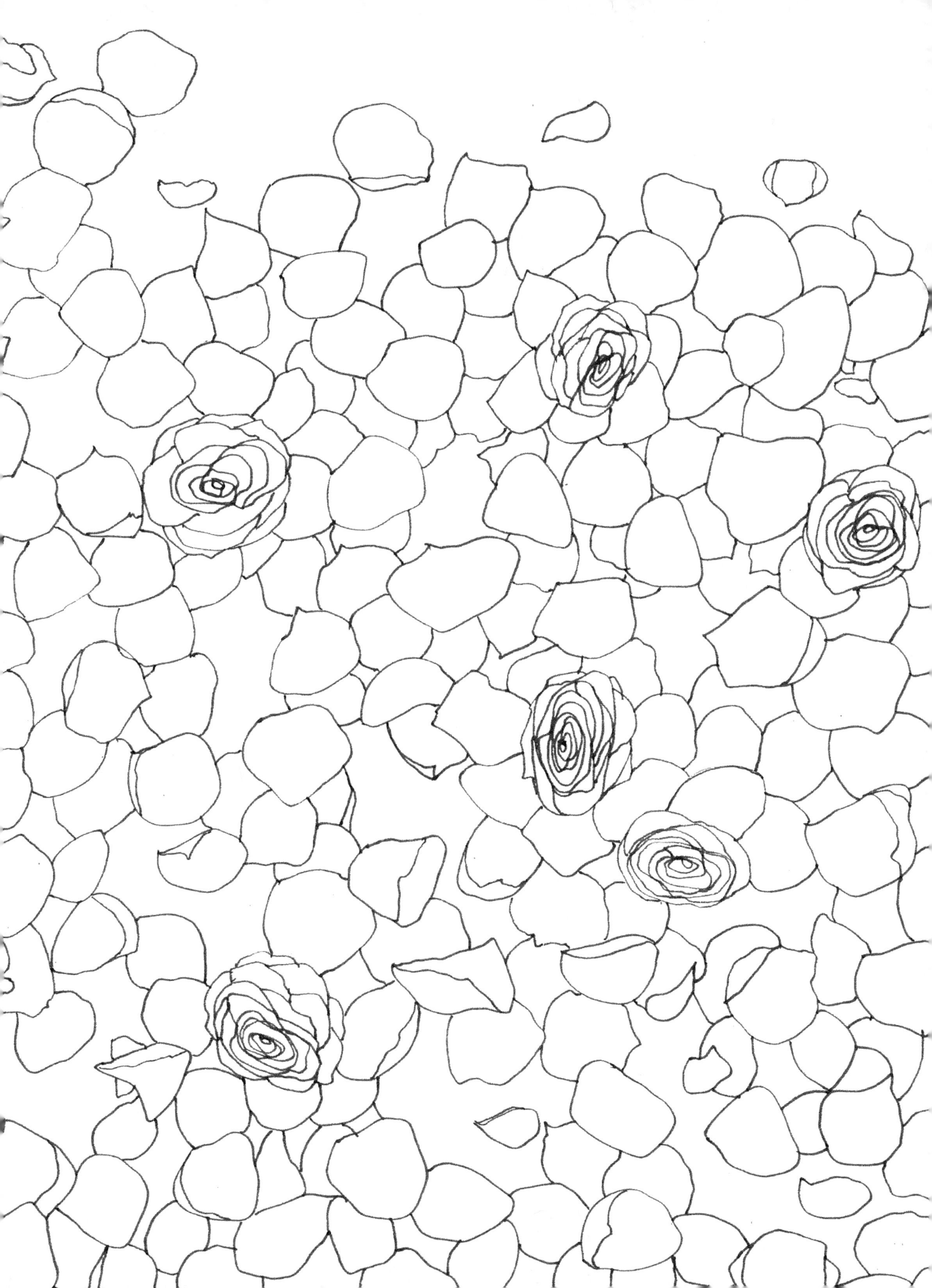

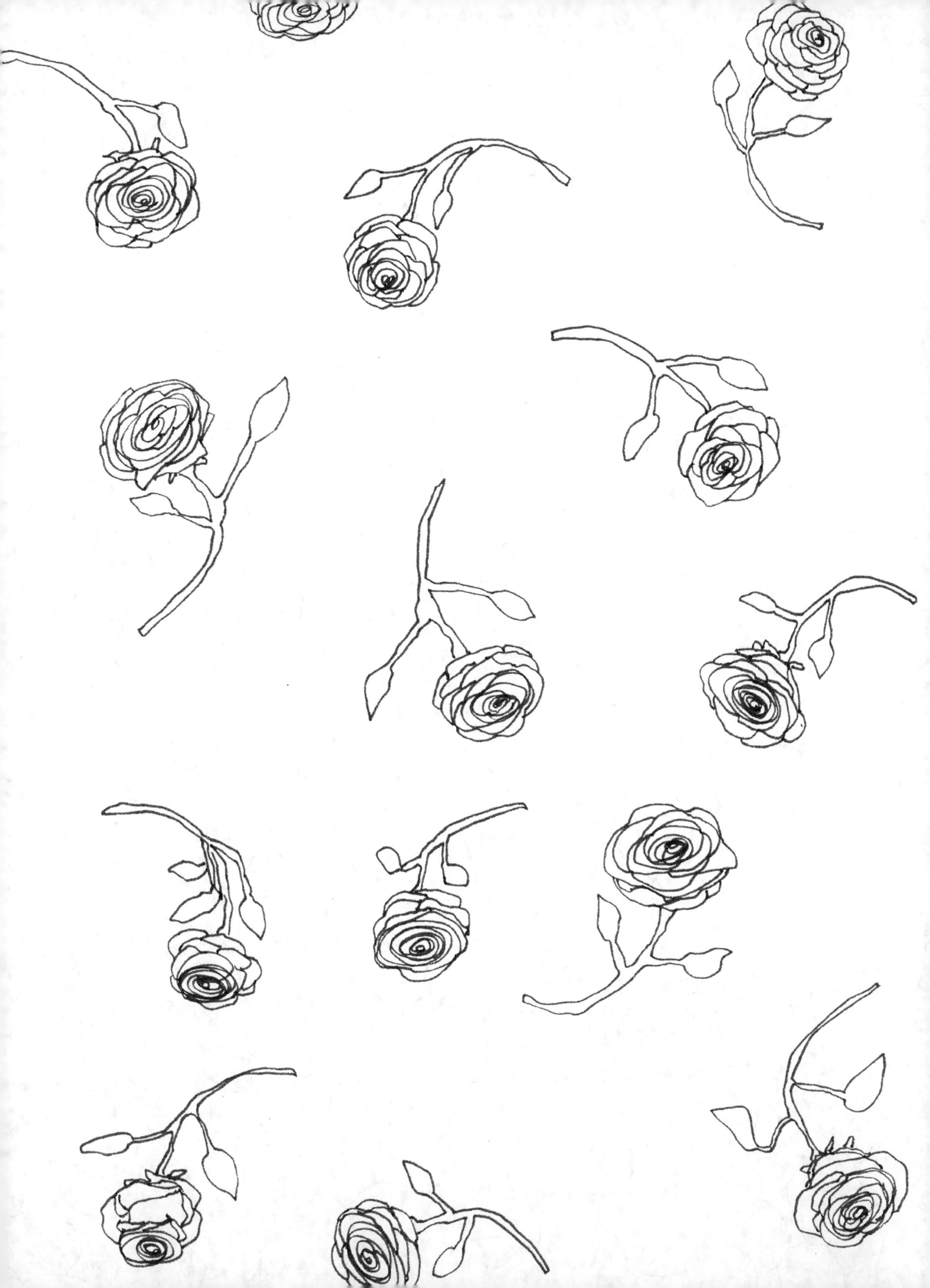

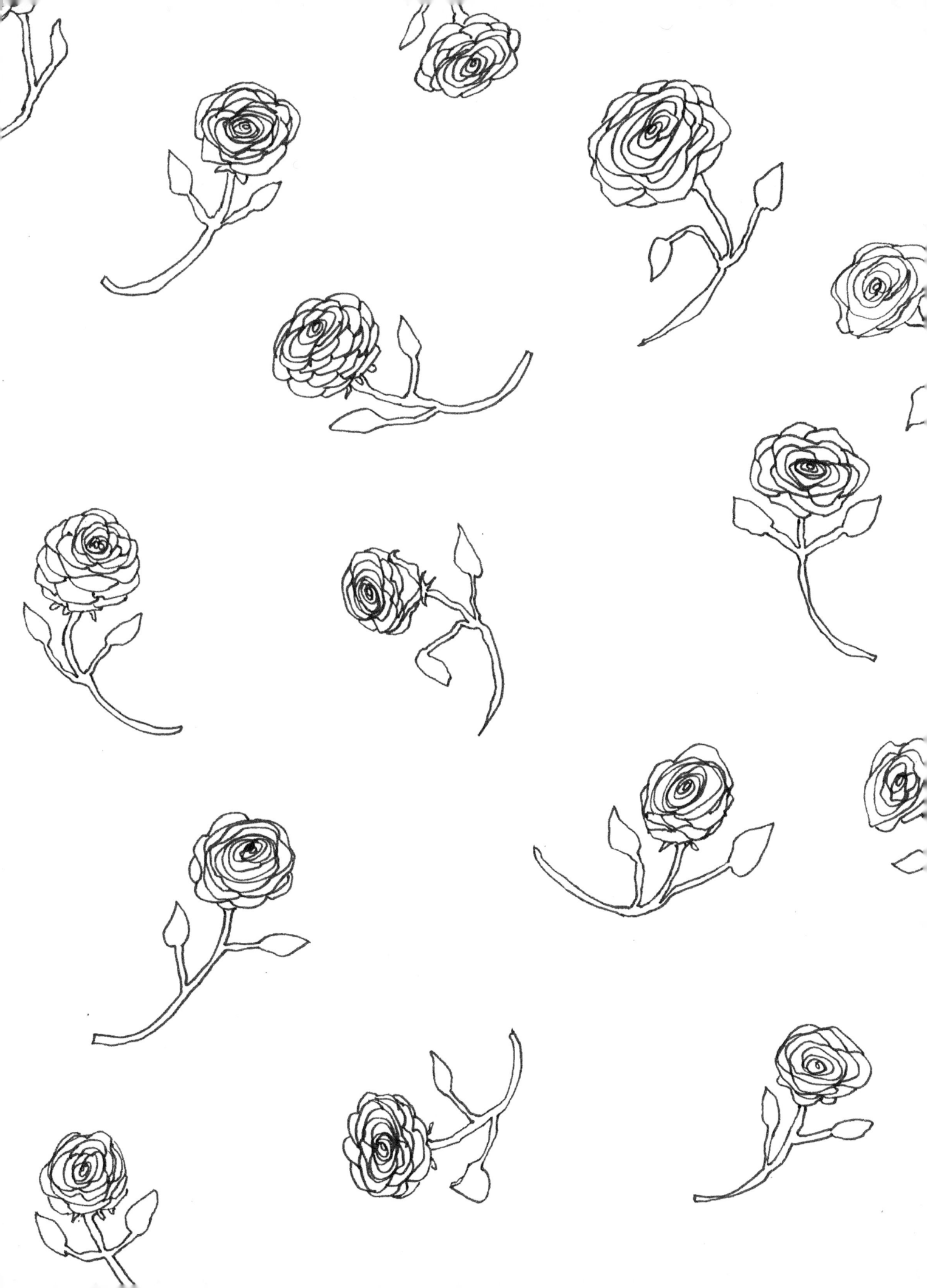

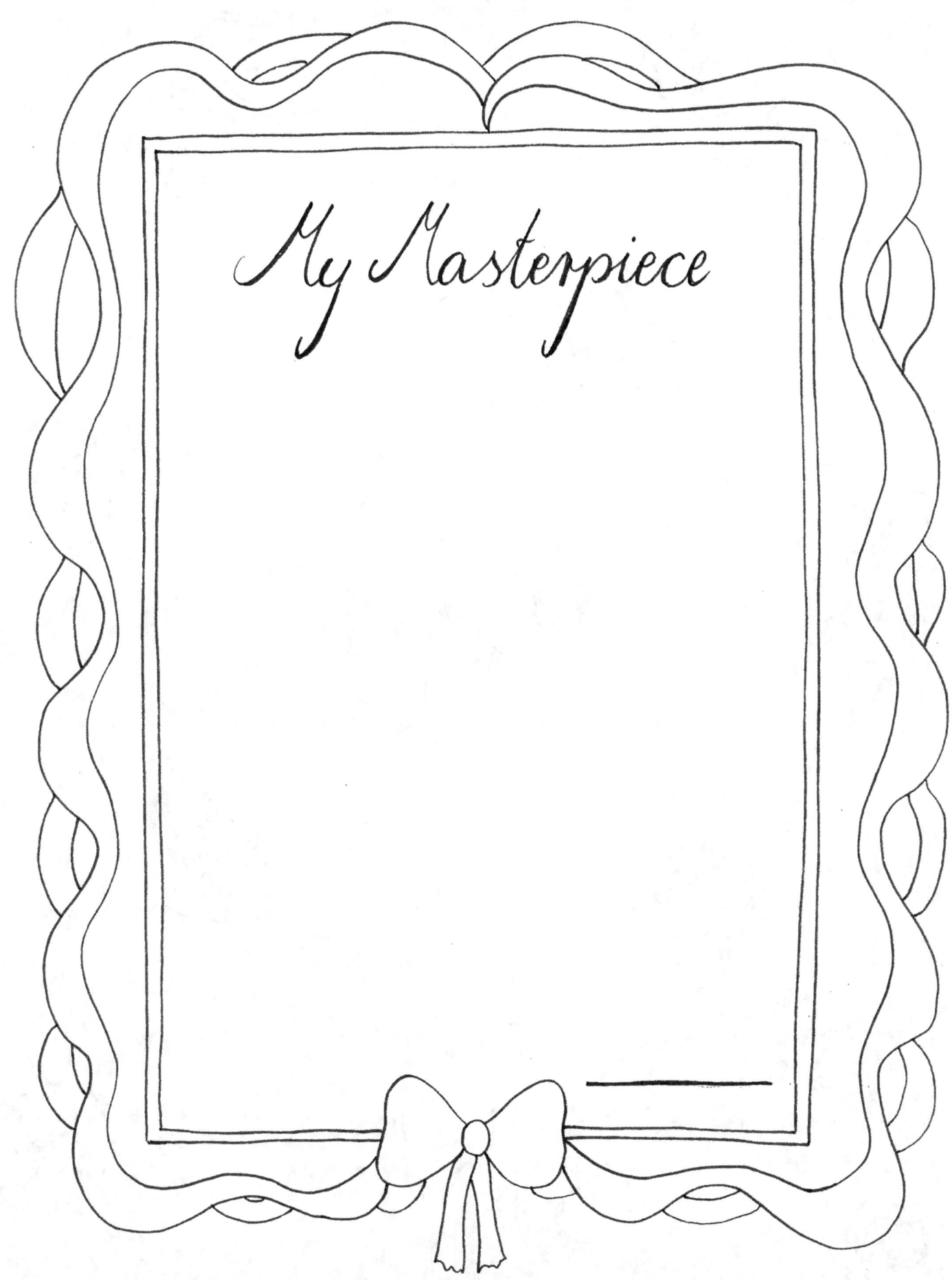

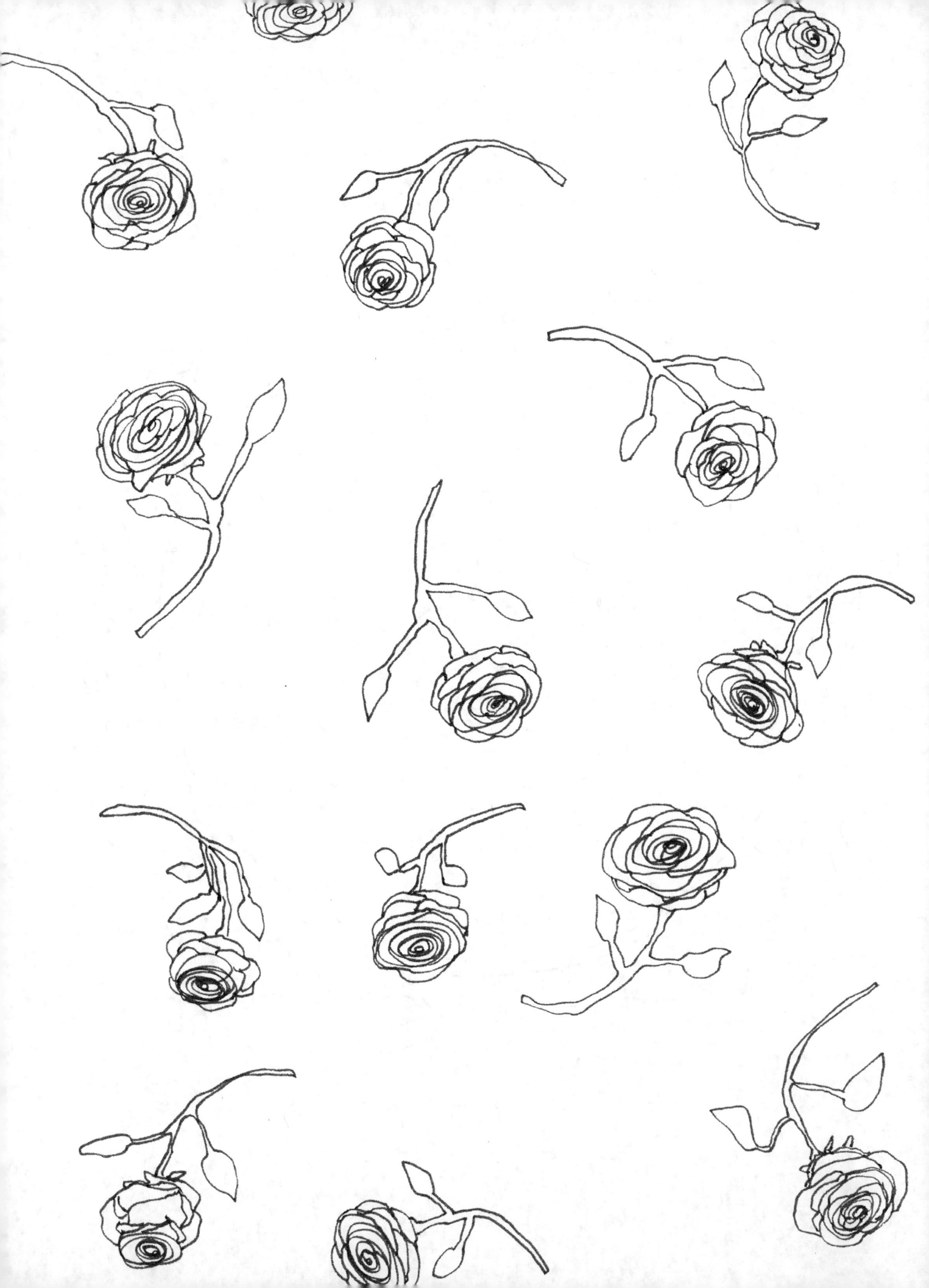

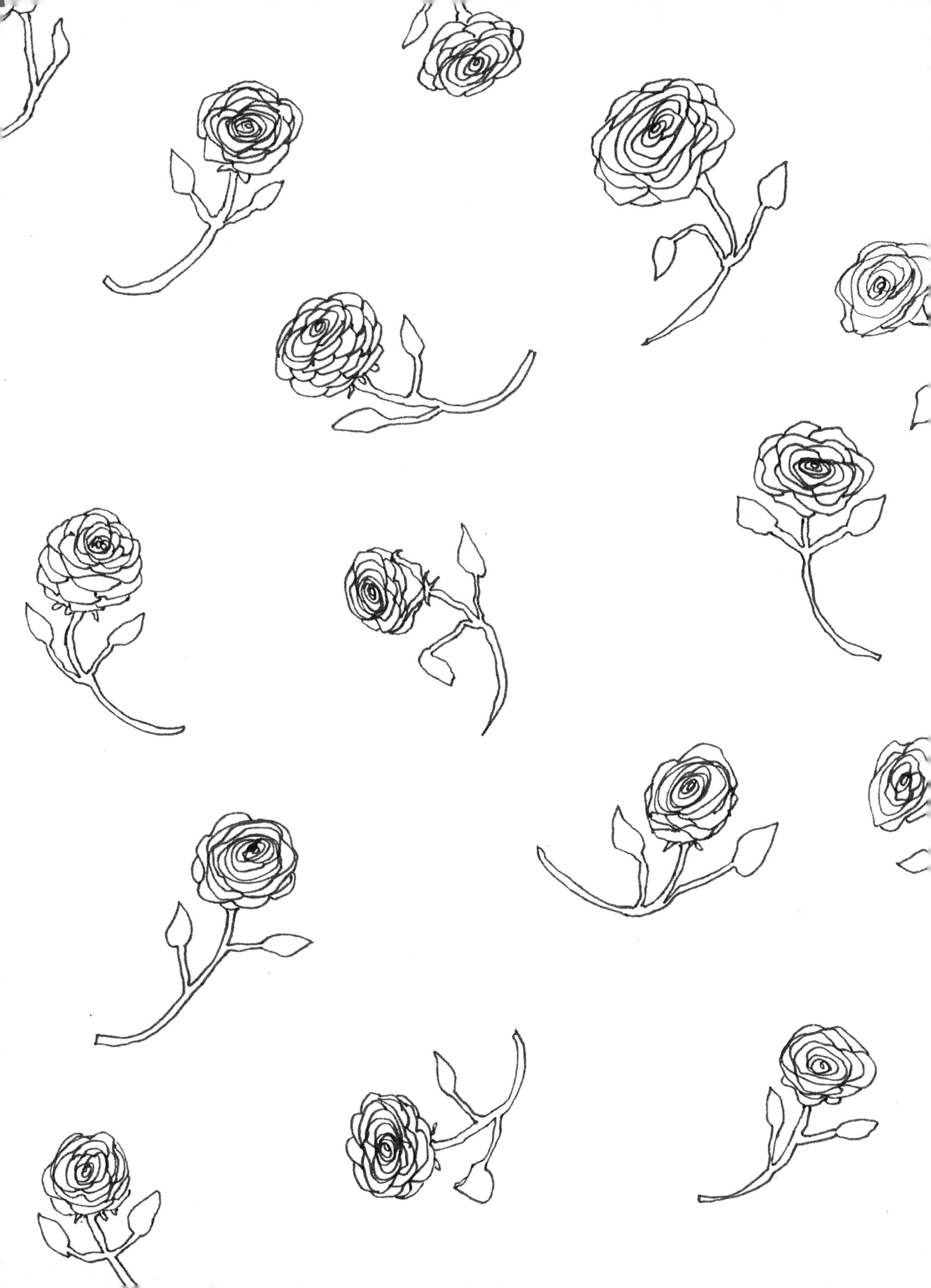

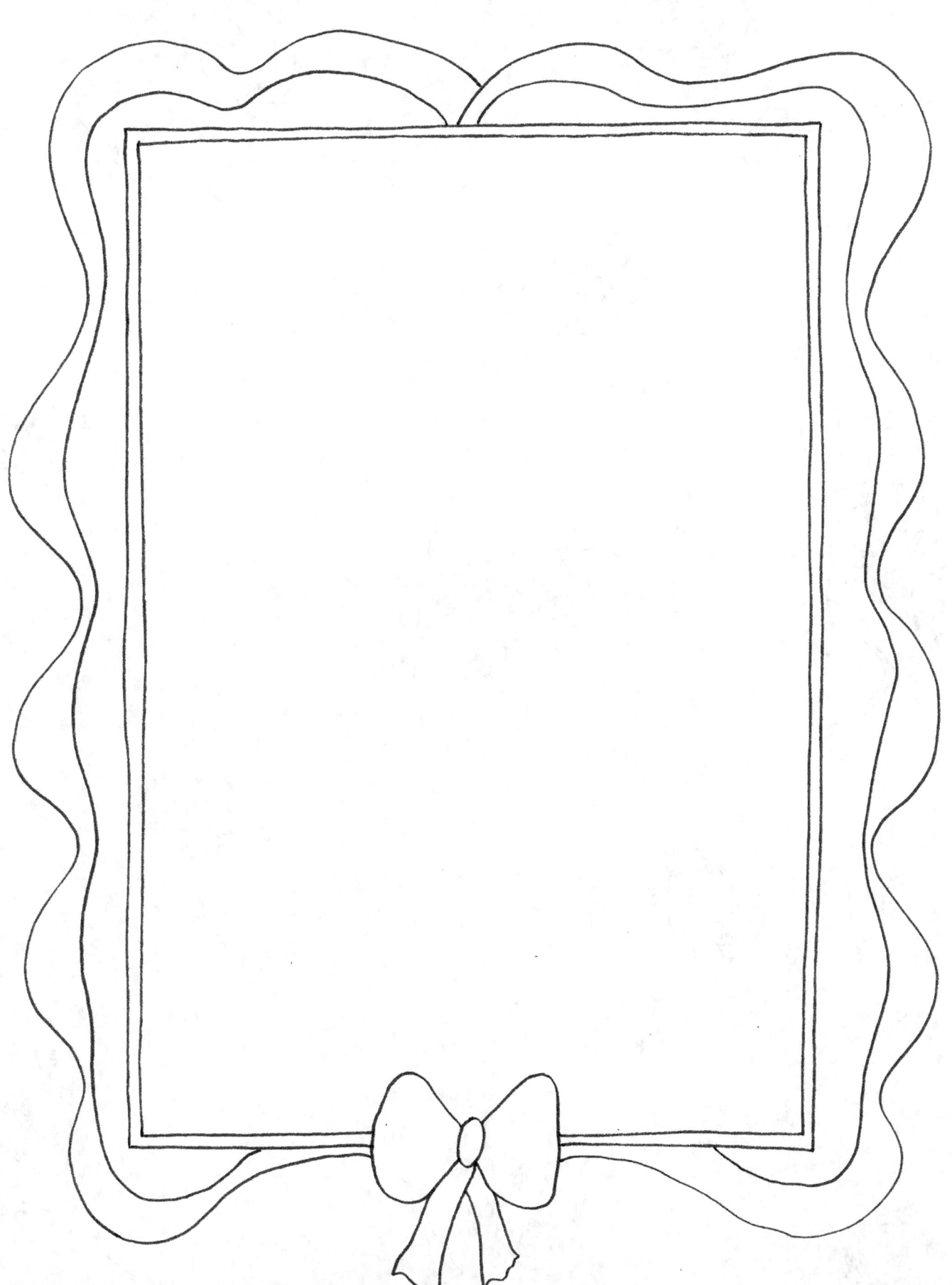

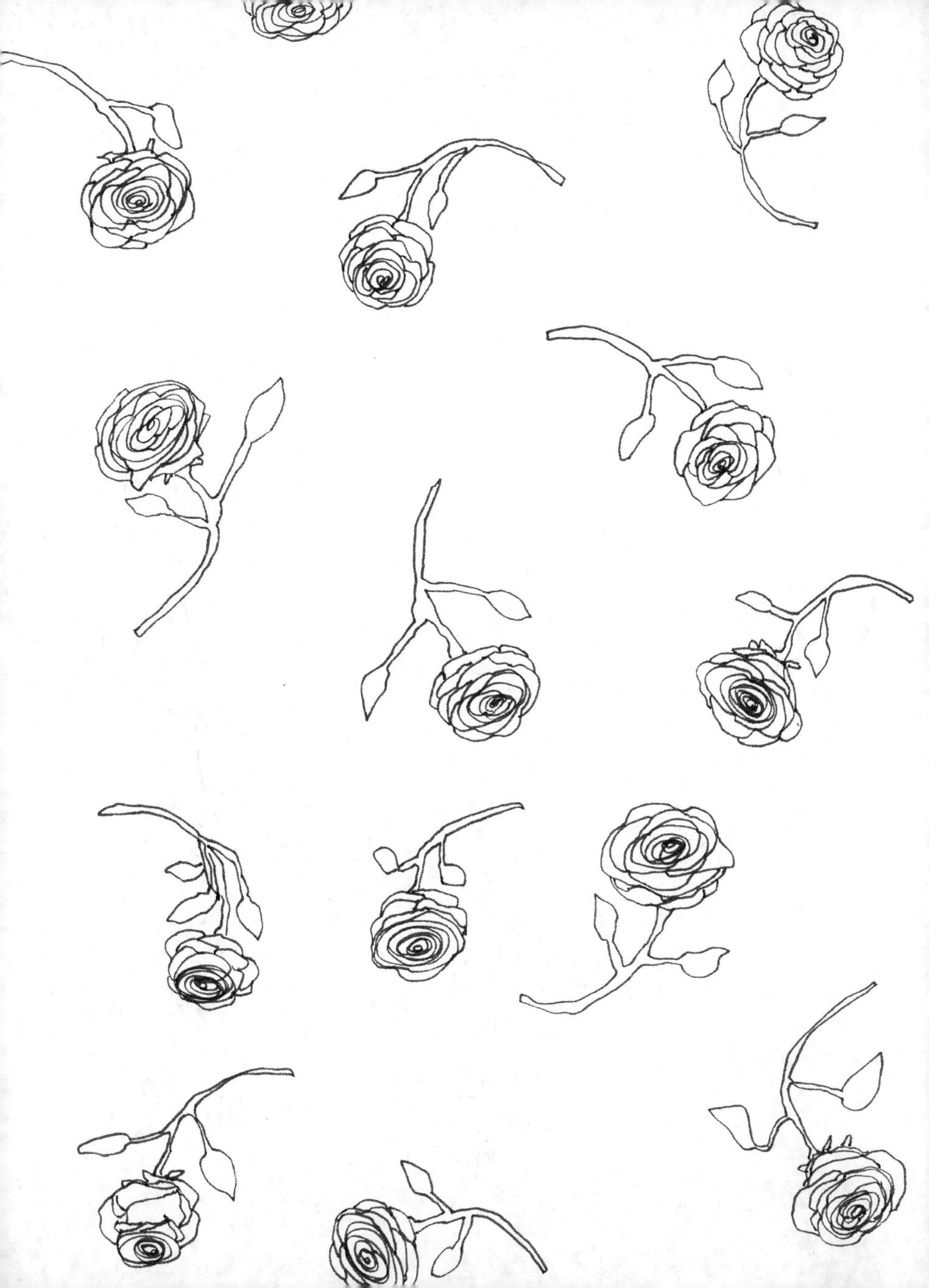

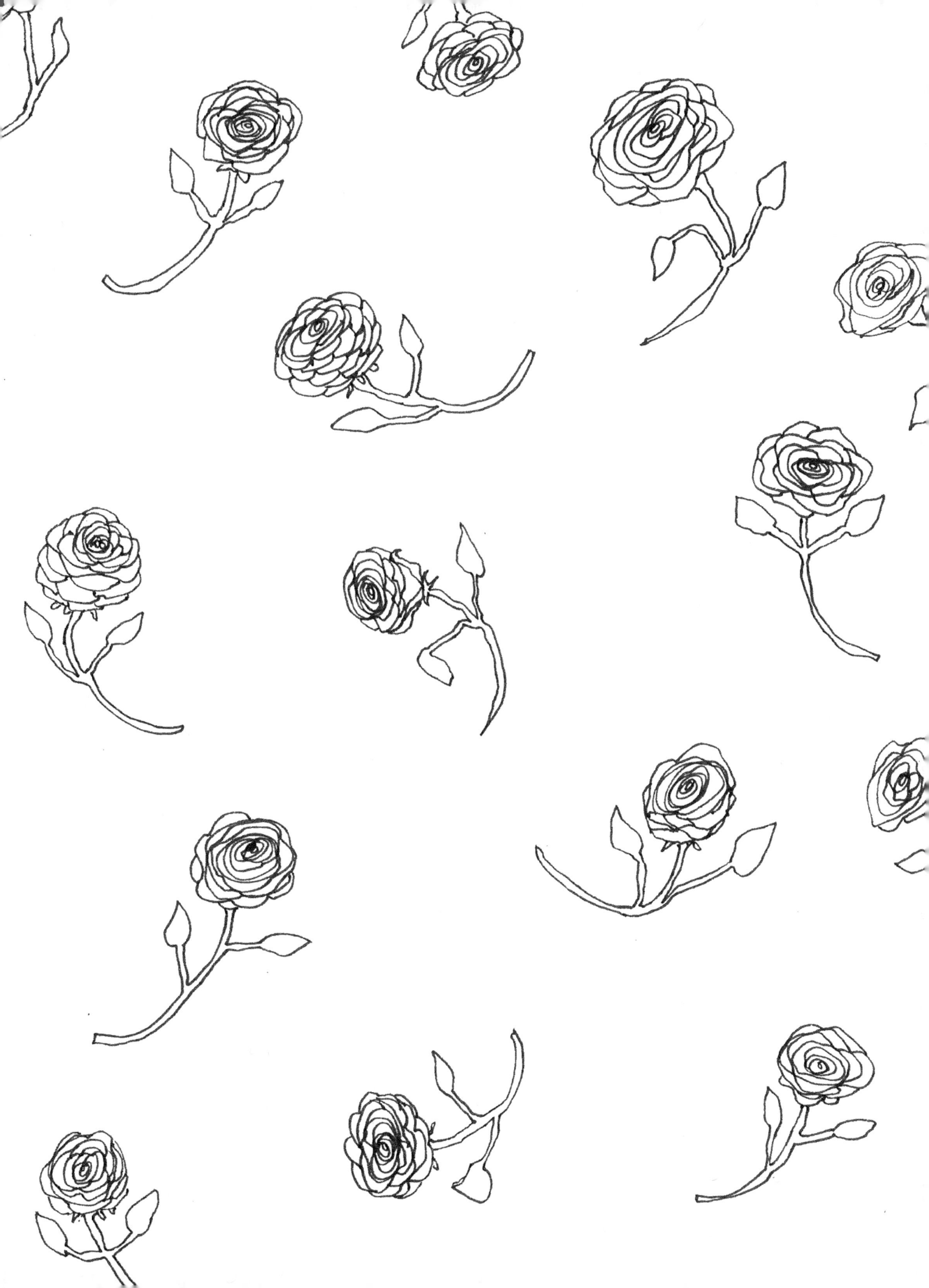

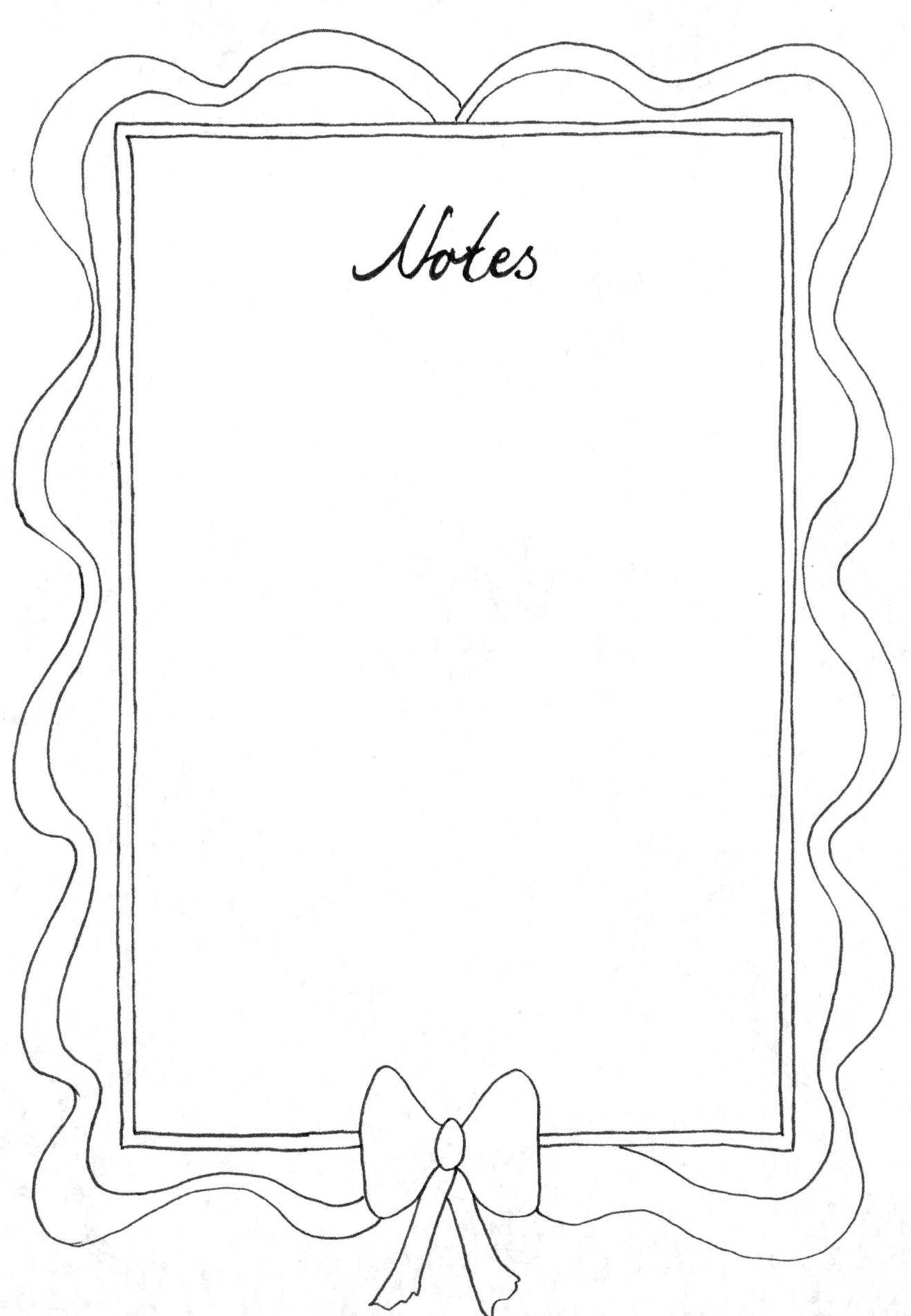

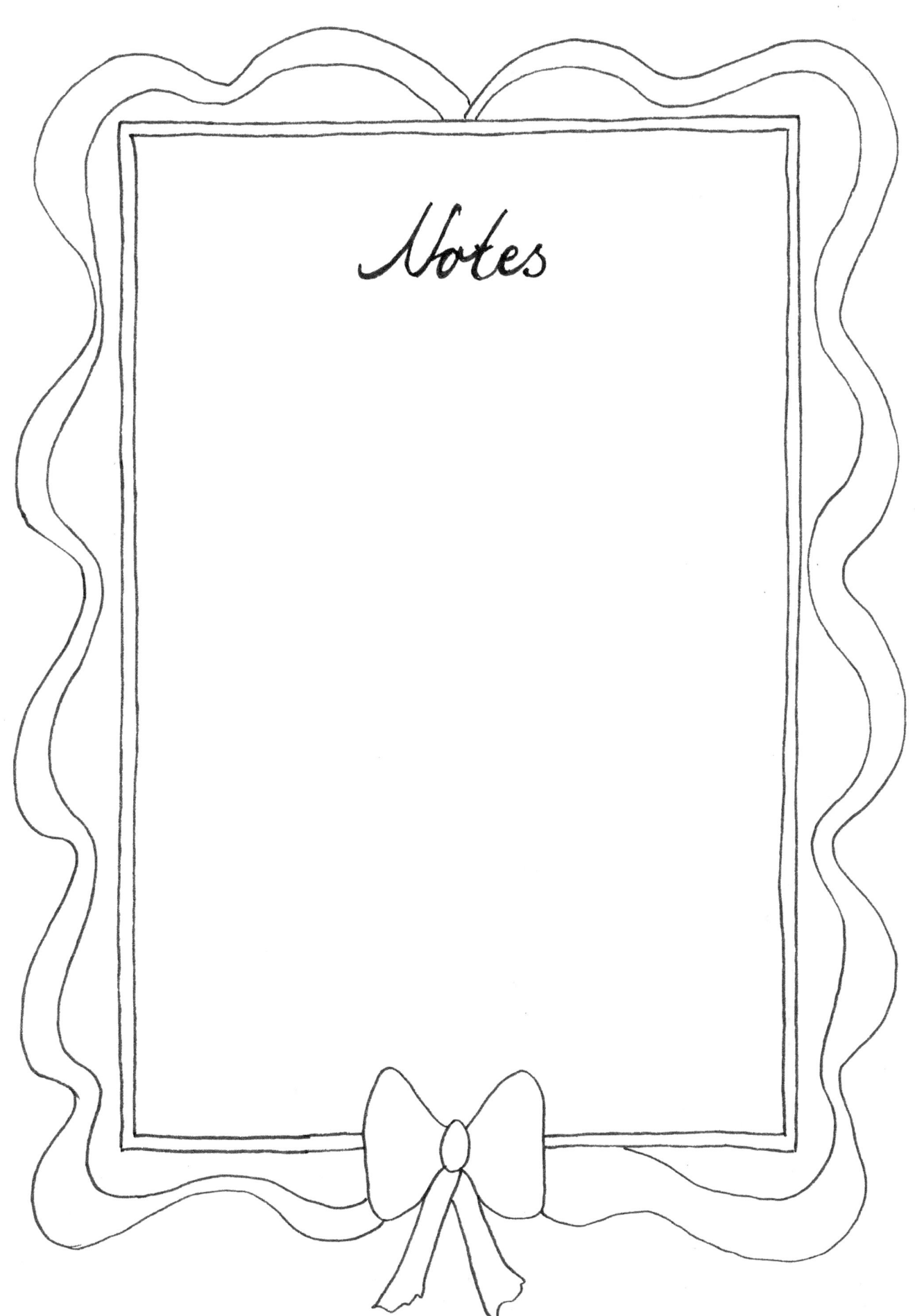

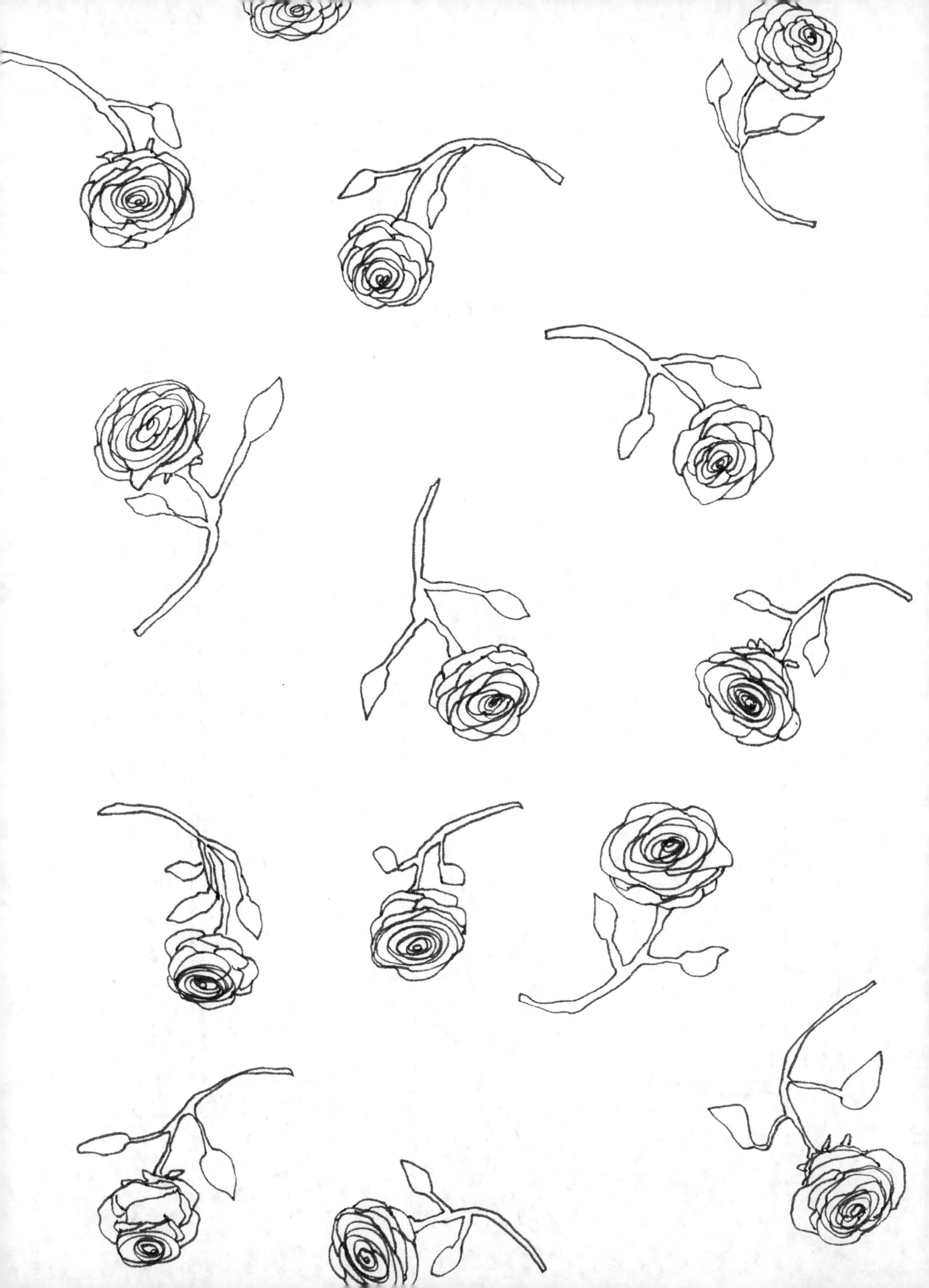

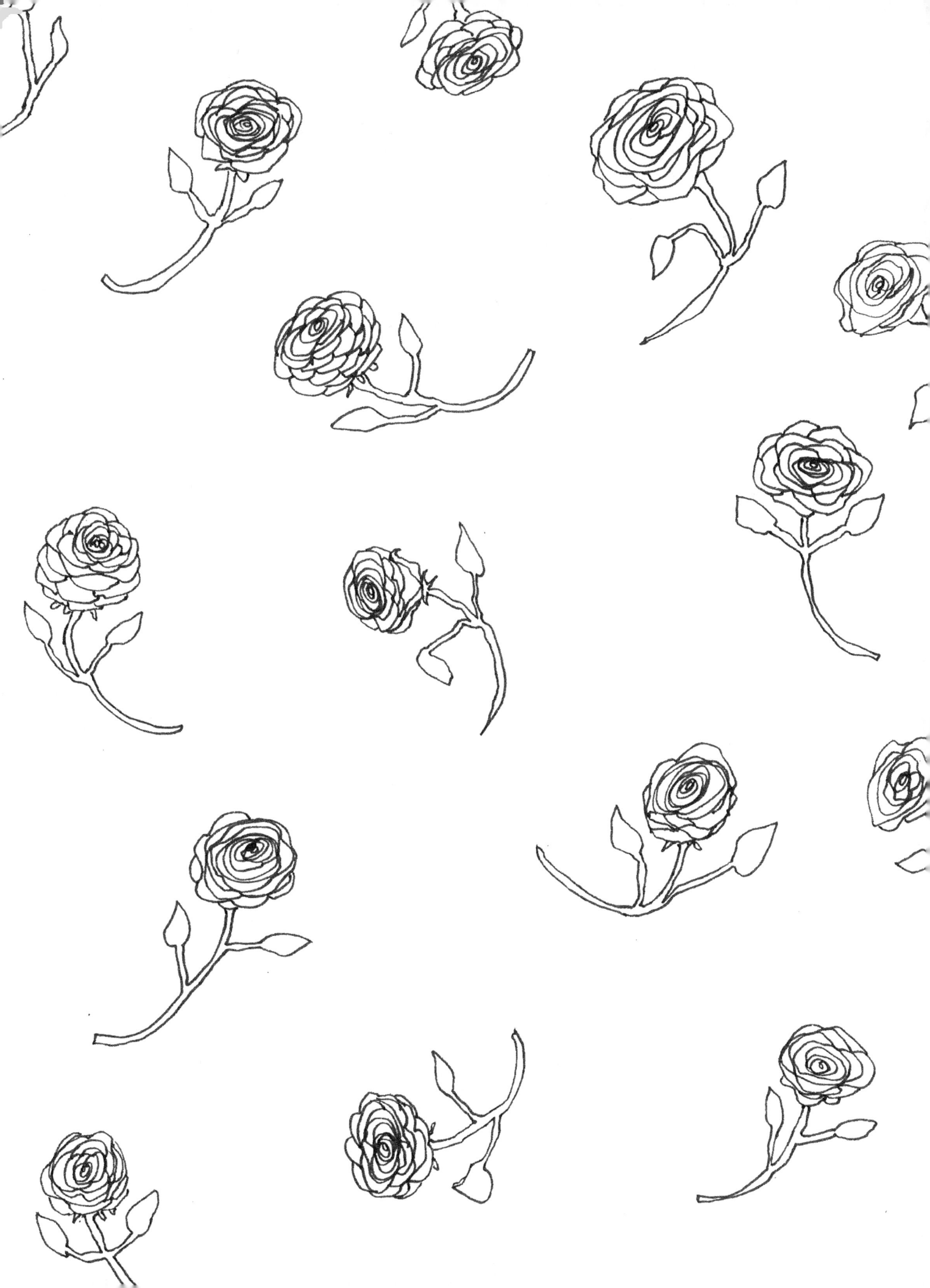

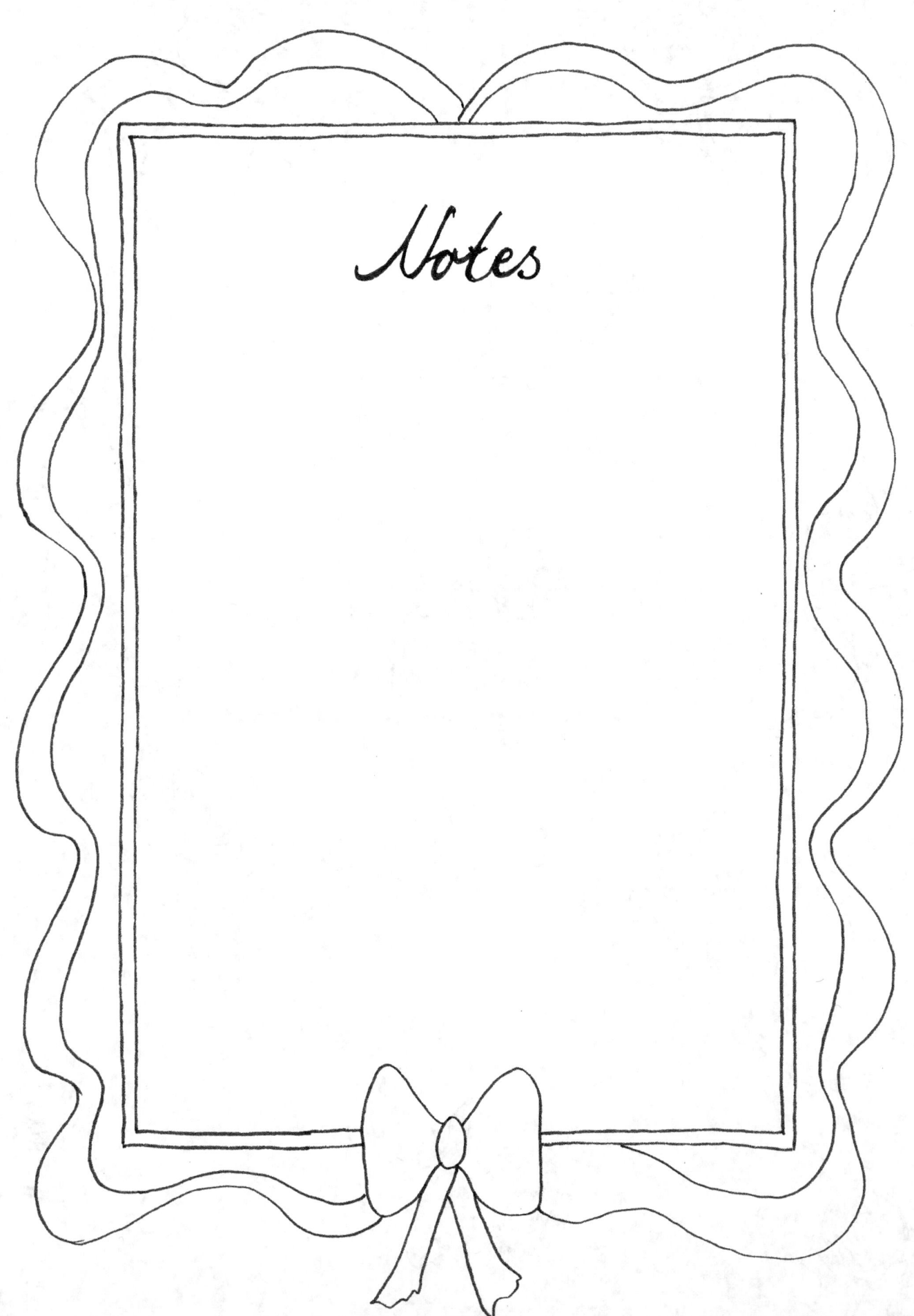

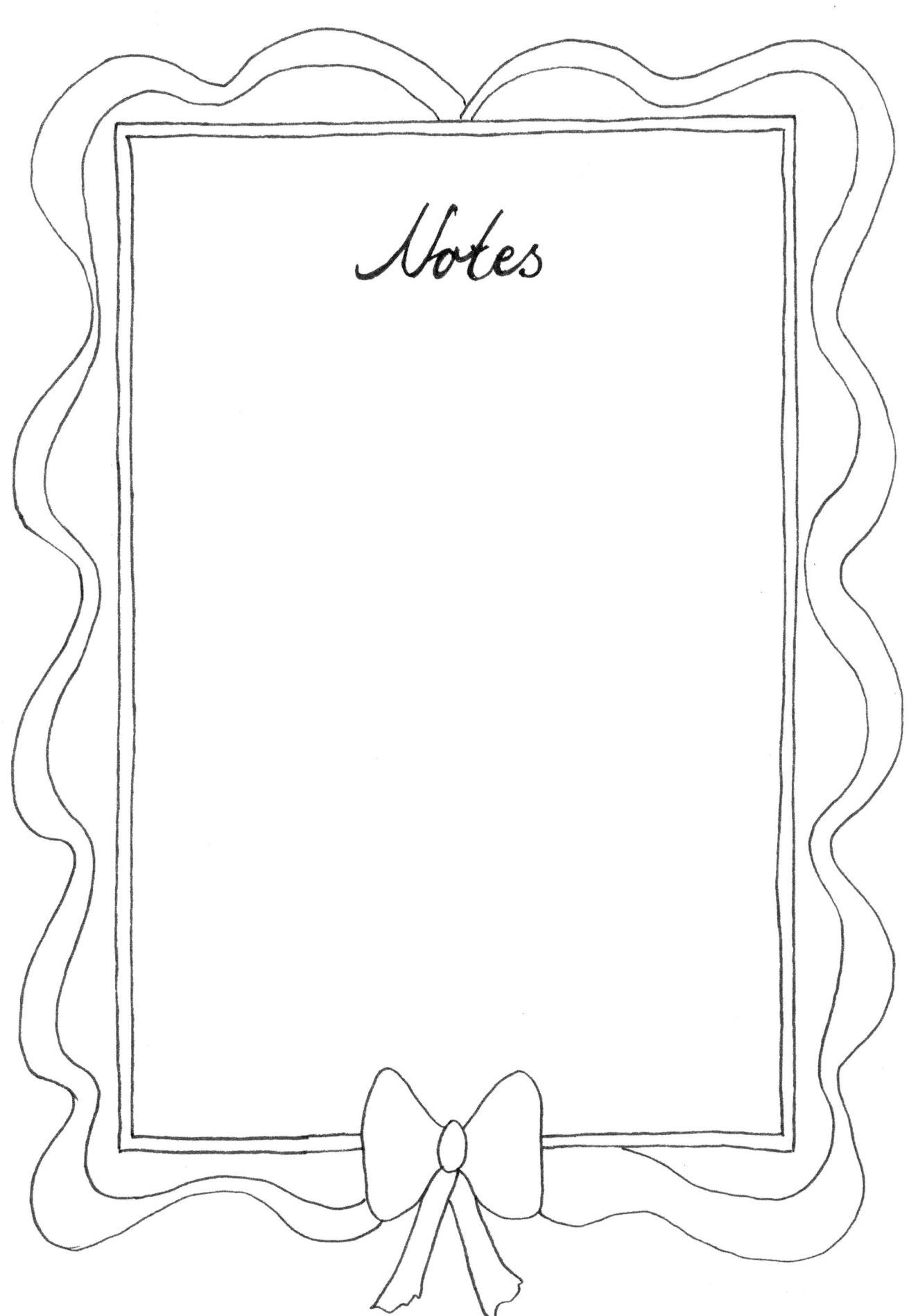

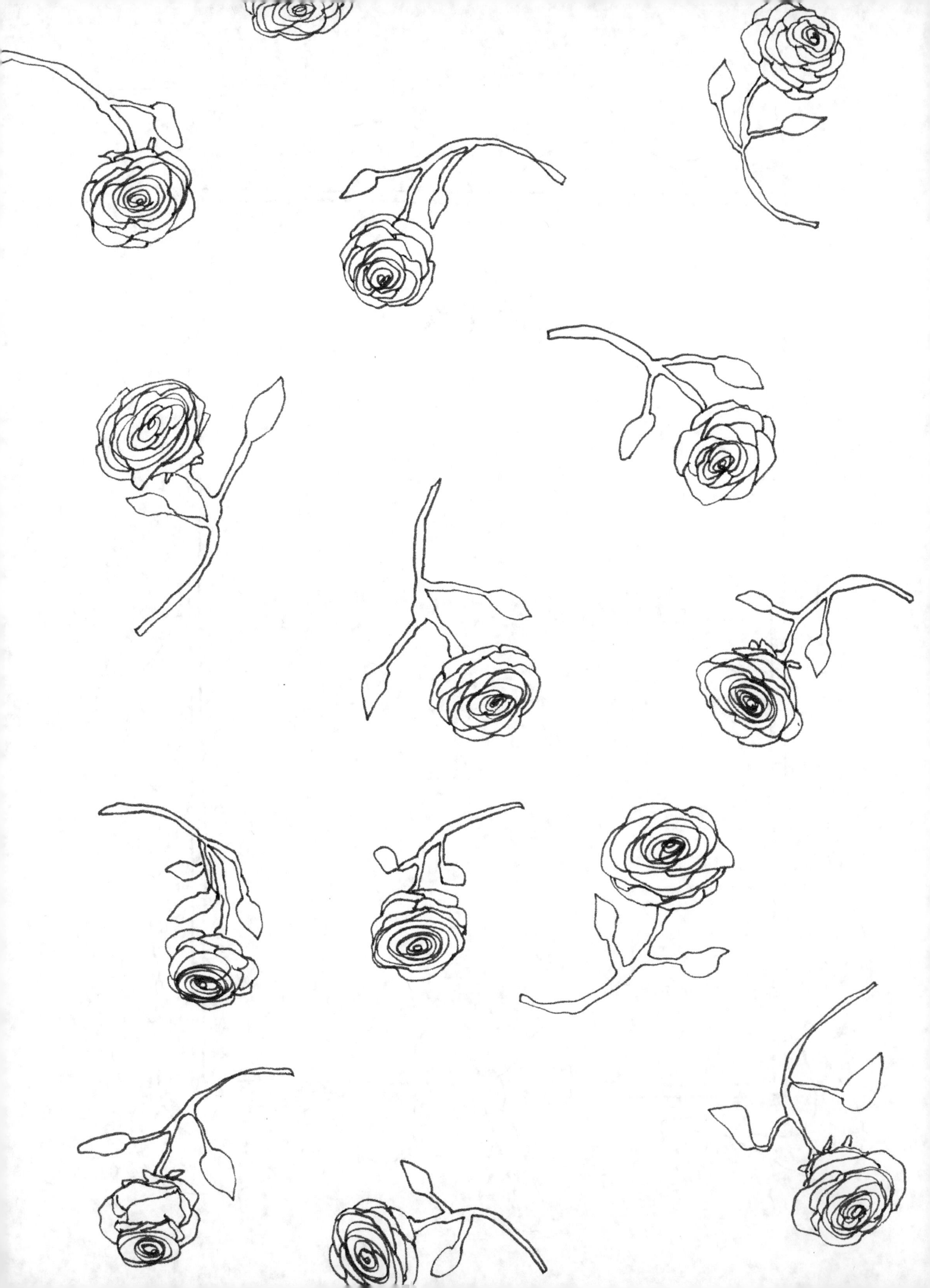

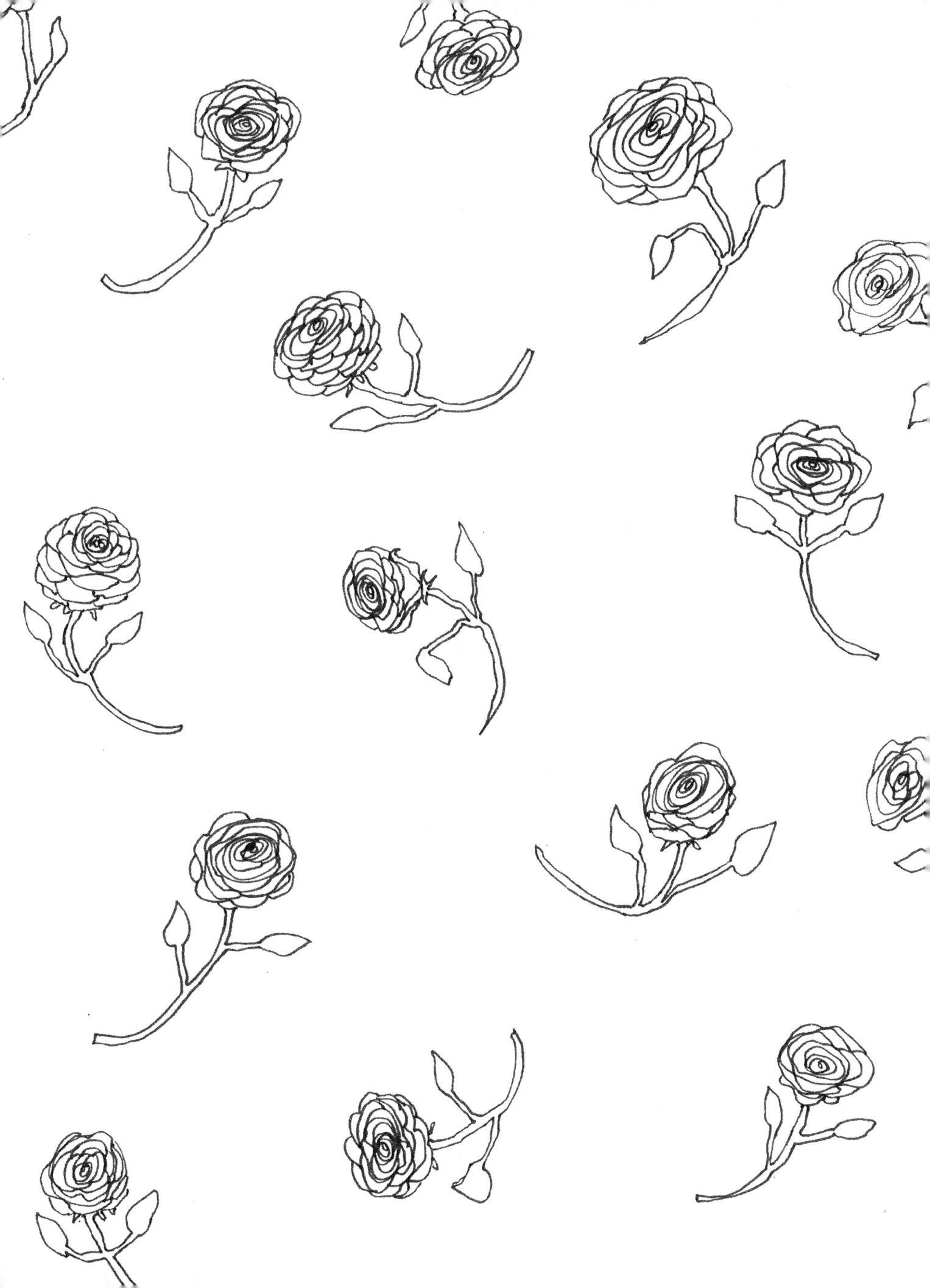

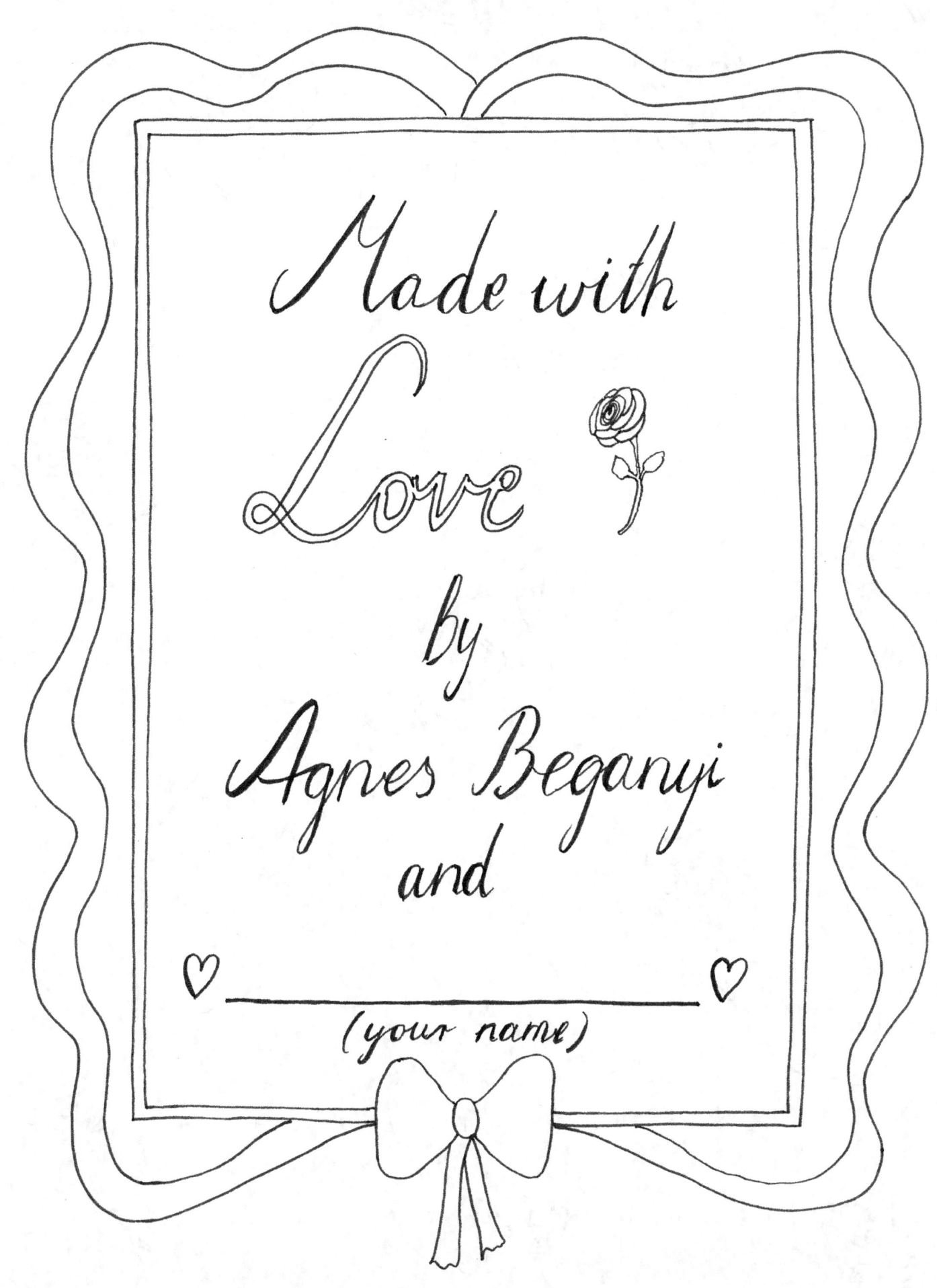

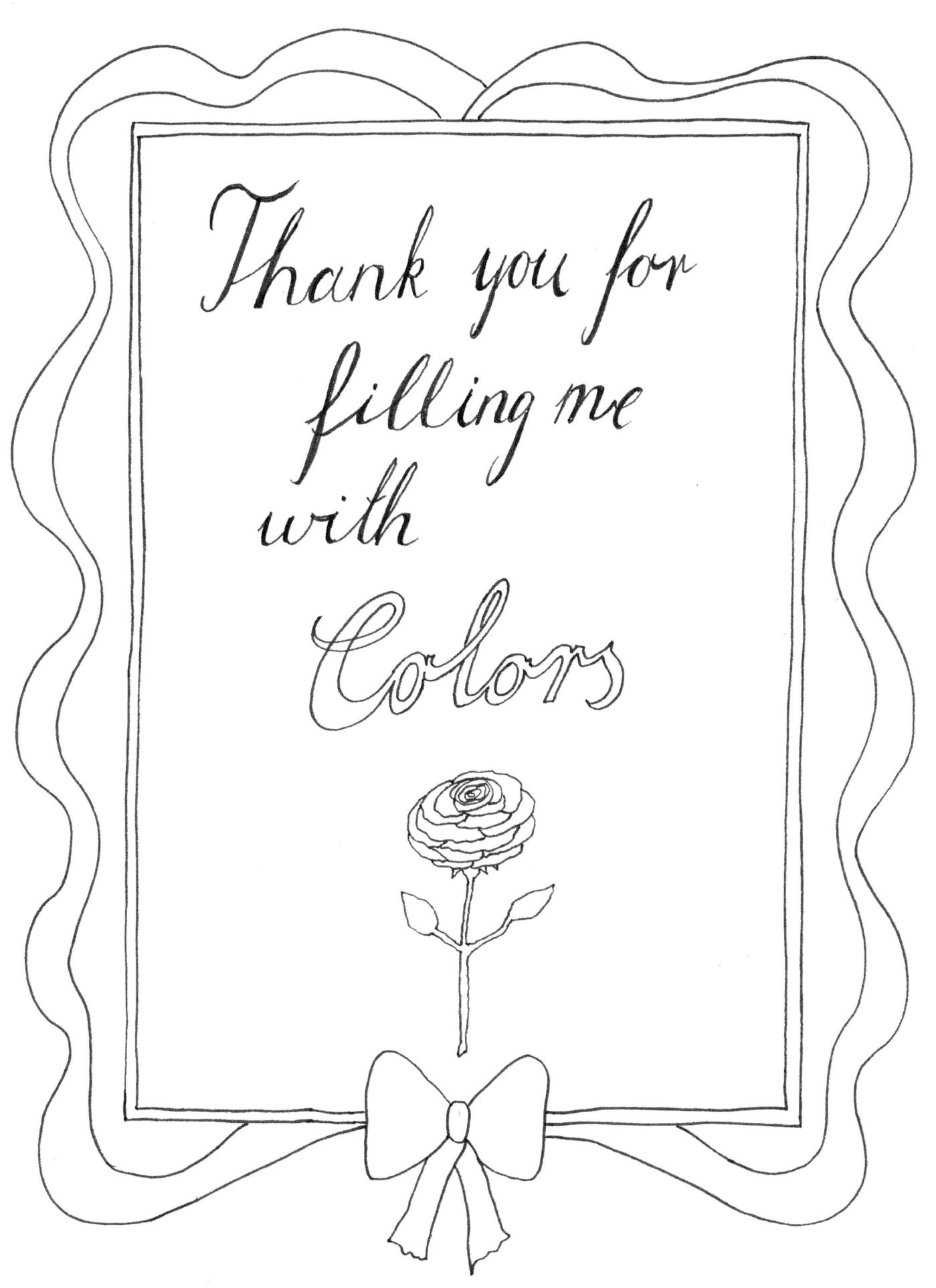

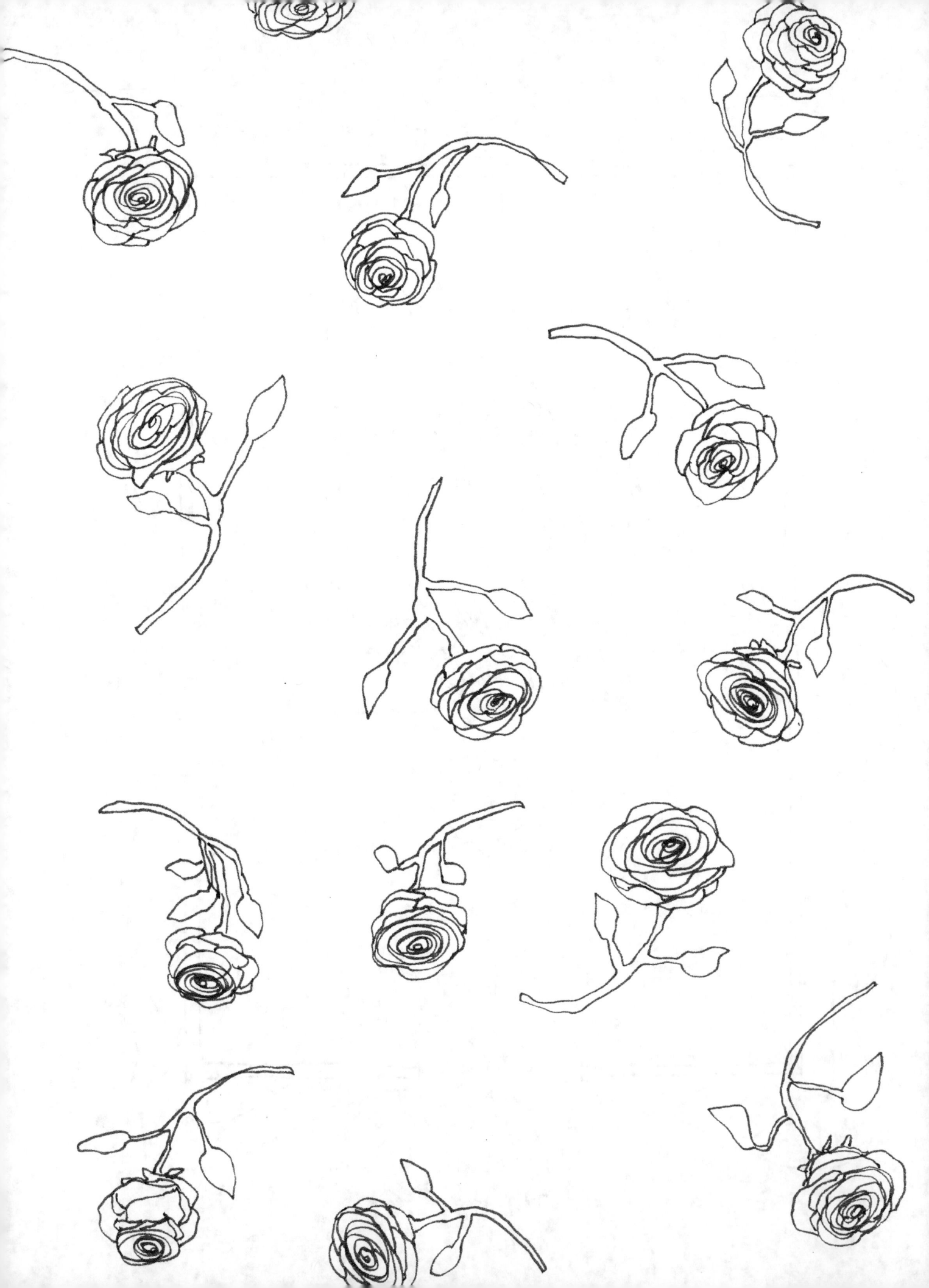

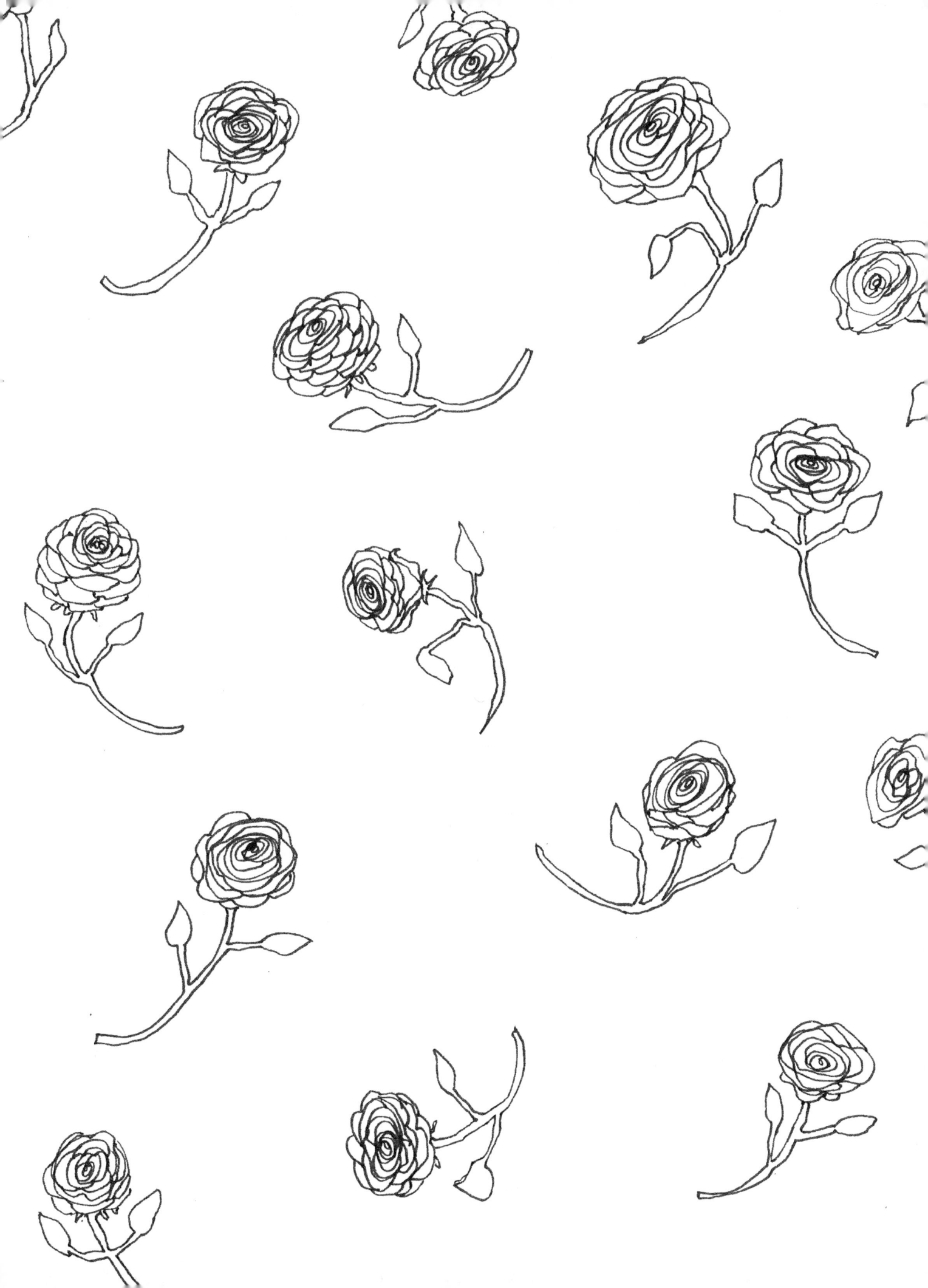

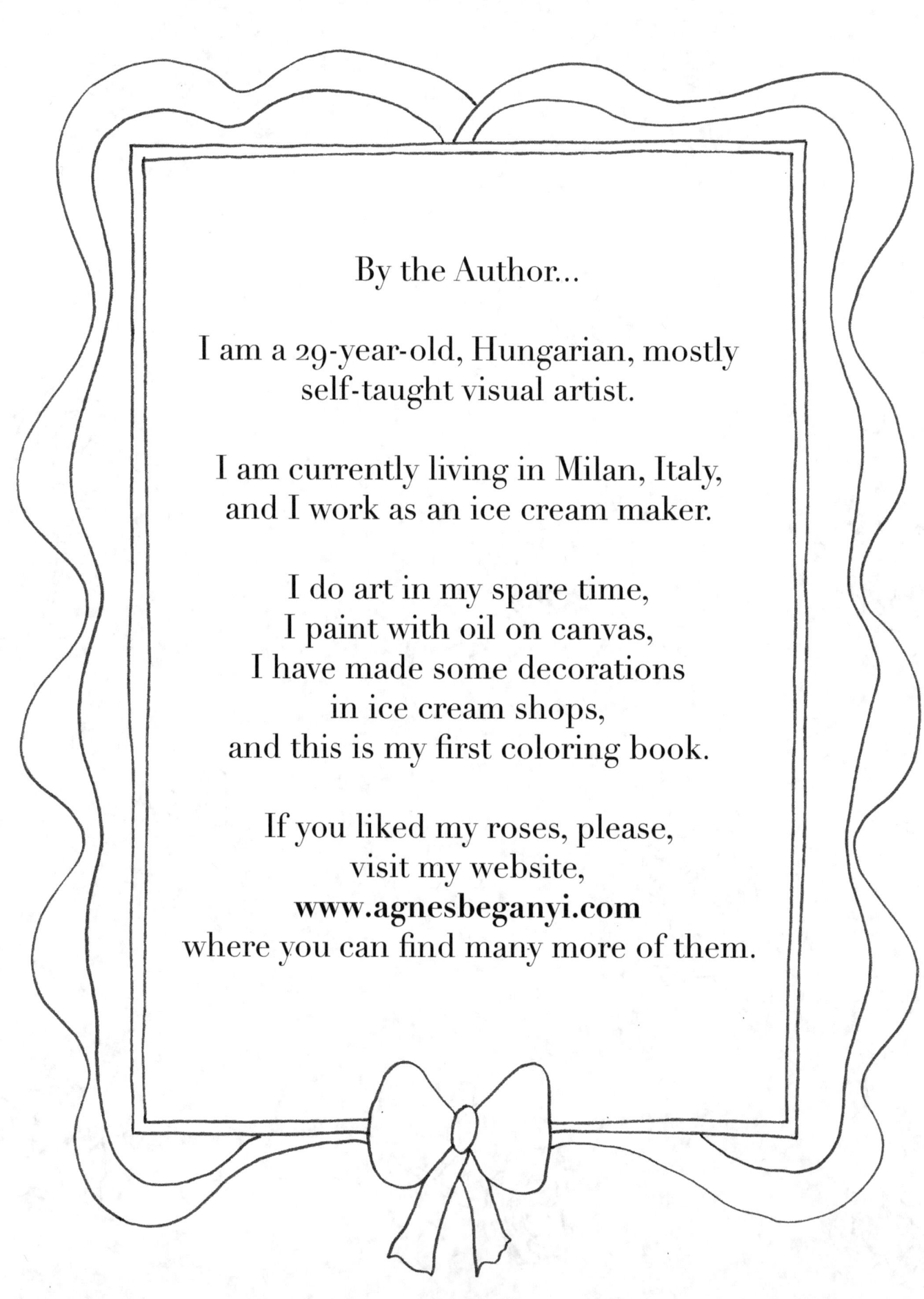

By the Author...

I am a 29-year-old, Hungarian, mostly
self-taught visual artist.

I am currently living in Milan, Italy,
and I work as an ice cream maker.

I do art in my spare time,
I paint with oil on canvas,
I have made some decorations
in ice cream shops,
and this is my first coloring book.

If you liked my roses, please,
visit my website,
www.agnesbeganyi.com
where you can find many more of them.

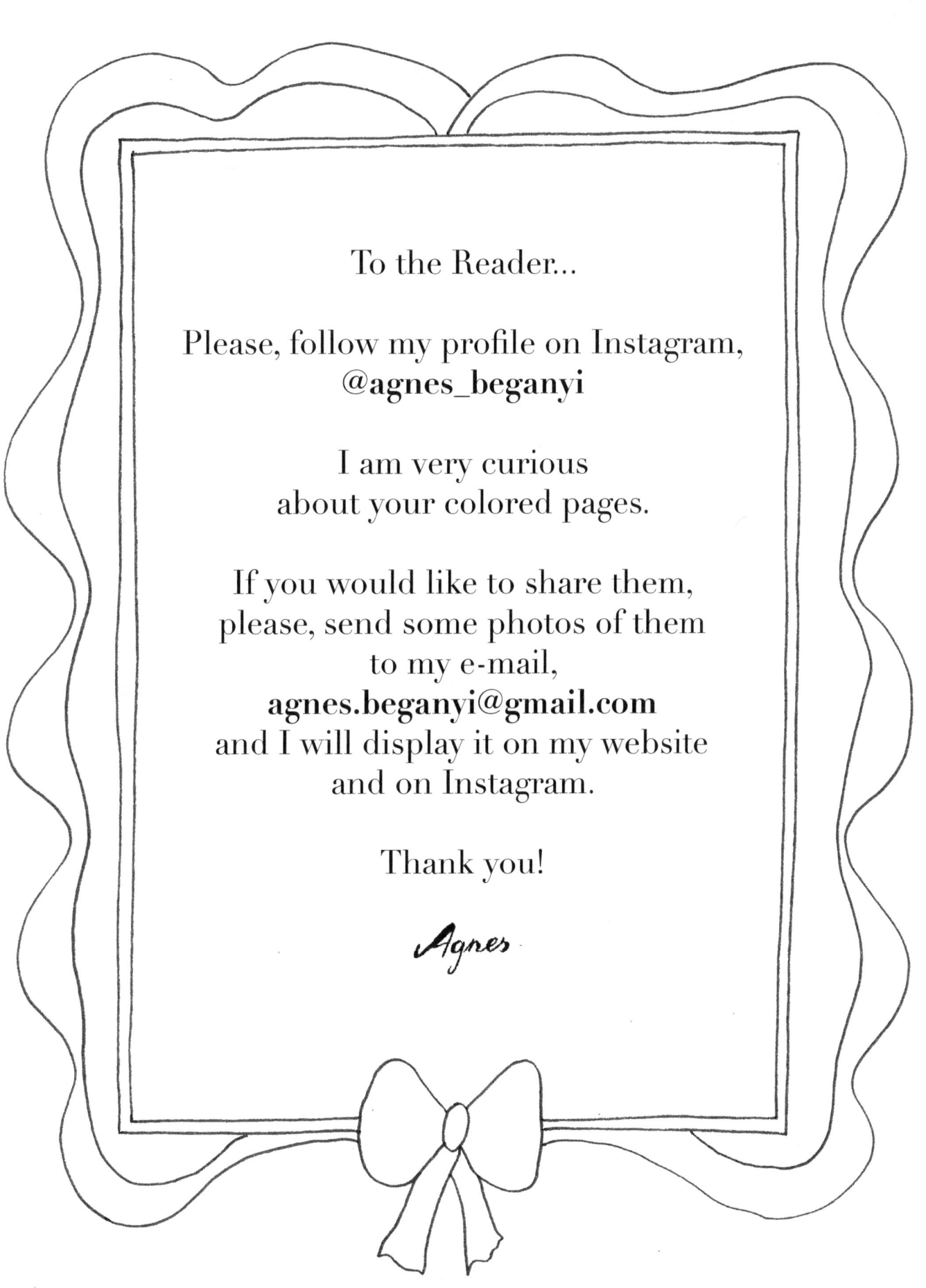

To the Reader...

Please, follow my profile on Instagram,
@agnes_beganyi

I am very curious
about your colored pages.

If you would like to share them,
please, send some photos of them
to my e-mail,
agnes.beganyi@gmail.com
and I will display it on my website
and on Instagram.

Thank you!

Agnes

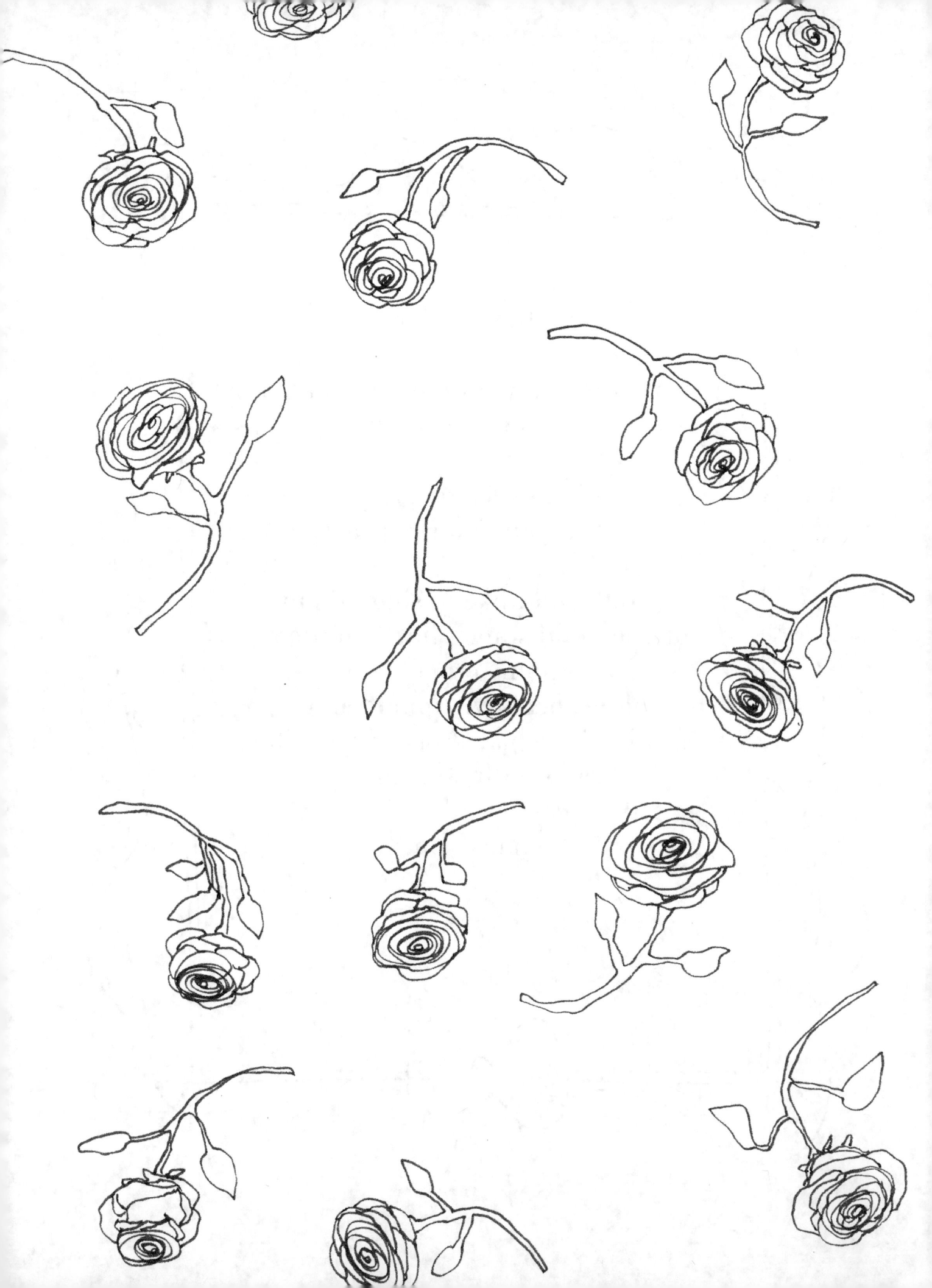

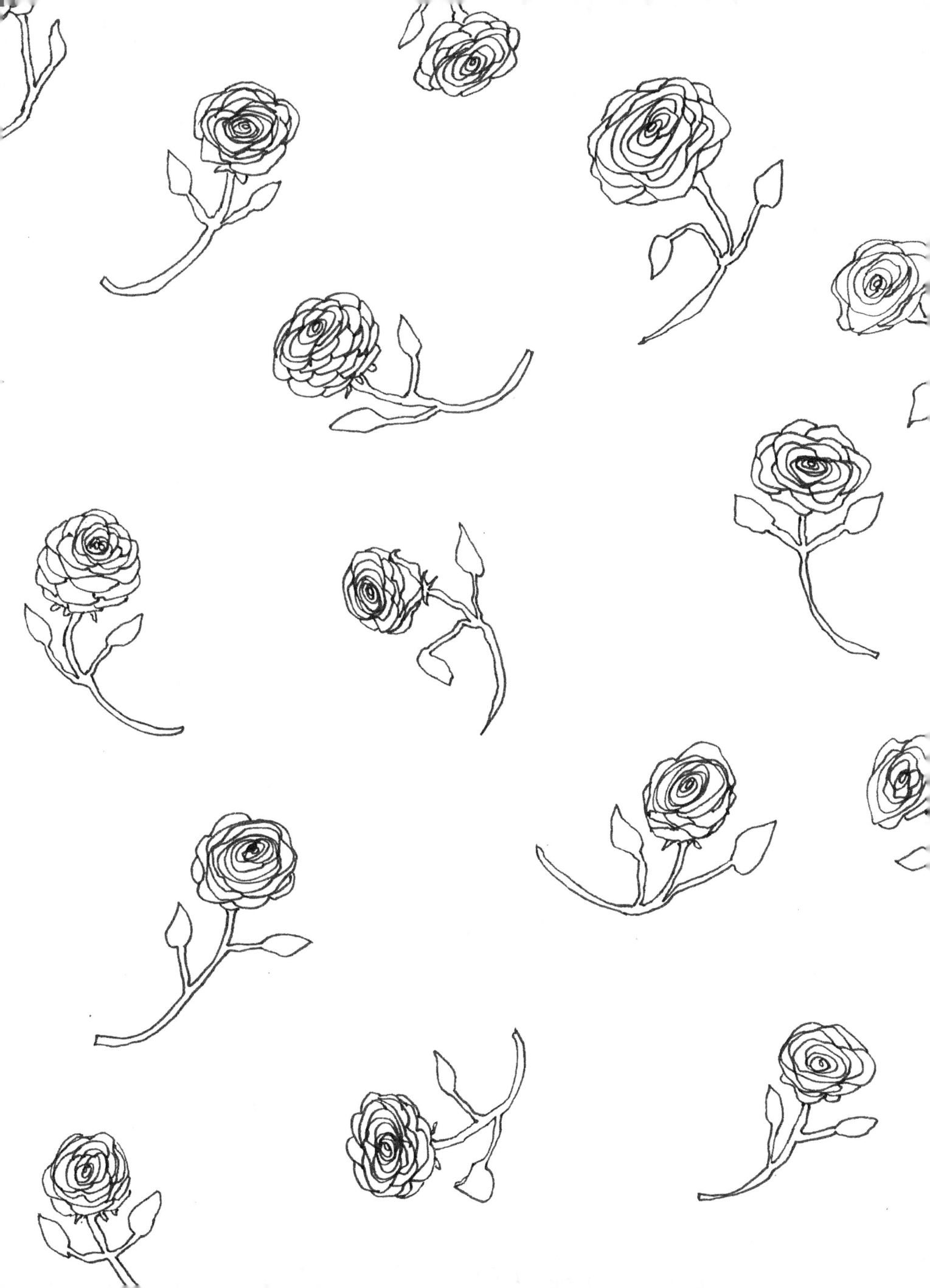

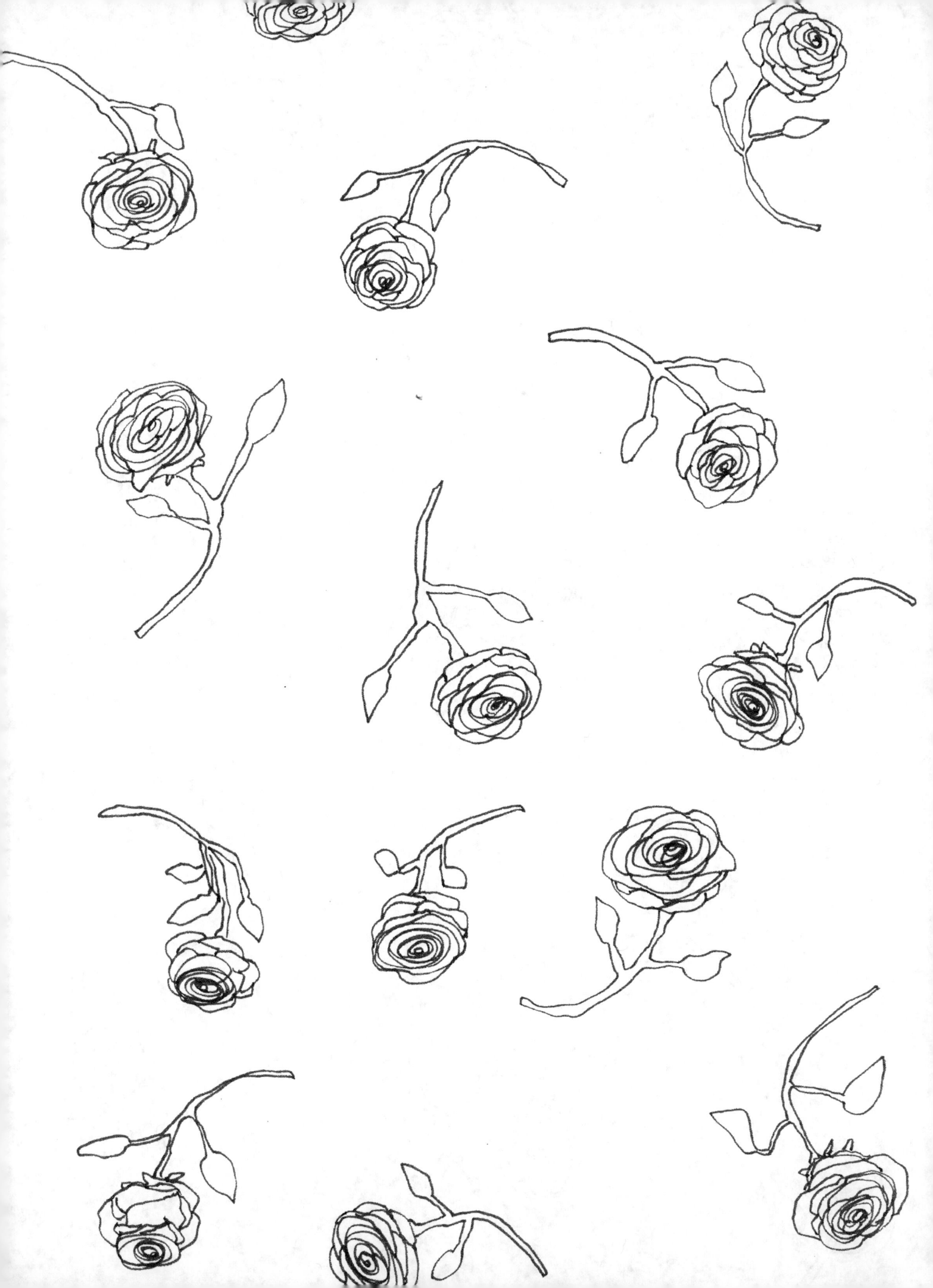